CW01660695

A BRIEF HISTORY OF SEVENTH-DAY ADVENTISTS

THIRD EDITION

Other books by George R. Knight (selected)

A.T. Jones: Point Man on Adventism's Charismatic Frontier
The Apocalyptic Vision and the Neutering of Adventism
The Cross of Christ
I Used to Be Perfect (Andrews University Press)
If I Were the Devil
Joseph Bates: The Real Founder of Seventh-day Adventism
Lest We Forget
Myths in Adventism
Sin and Salvation
A User-friendly Guide to the 1888 Message
William Miller and the Rise of Adventism (Pacific Press)

Books in the Adventist Heritage series

A Brief History of Seventh-day Adventists
A Search for Identity: The Development of Seventh-day Adventist Beliefs
Organizing for Mission and Growth: The Development of Adventist Church Structure

Books in the Ellen White series

Ellen White's World
Meeting Ellen White
Reading Ellen White
Walking With Ellen White

Books in the Exploring Commentary series

Exploring Ecclesiastes and Song of Solomon
Exploring Galatians and Ephesians
Exploring Hebrews
Exploring the Letters of John and Jude
Exploring Mark
Exploring Romans
Exploring Thessalonians

A study guide for each of the books in this series is available on www.adventistbookcenter.com

A Brief History of Seventh-day Adventists

Third Edition

George R. Knight

Review and Herald® Publishing Association
Since 1861 | www.reviewandherald.com

The author assumes full responsibility for the accuracy of all facts and quotations as cited in this book.

This book was
Edited by Gerald Wheeler
Copyedited by Jocelyn Fay and James Cavil
Designed by Bryan Gray/Genesis Design, LLC
Cover art direction and design by Ed Guthero
Cover illustration by Lars Justinen
Typeset: 11/14 Goudy

Printed by Pacific Press® Publishing Association
PRINTED IN U.S.A.

R&H Cataloging Service
Knight, George Raymond
A brief history of Seventh-day Adventists.

1. Seventh-day Adventists—History. I. Title.

286.732

ISBN 978-0-8280-1430-4

January 2019

Contents

Dedicated to
Richard Scull II, Heather Gambill,
Fallon Knight, Melanie Fusté and Roberto Fusté V
—Grandchildren All

List of Abbreviations

A&D	*Wm. Miller's Apology and Defence*
Adv. Rev.	*Adventist Review*
AH	*Advent Herald*
AR	*Advent Review*
AS	*American Sentinel of Religious Liberty*
CTemp	*Christian Temperance and Bible Hygiene*, by James White and Ellen G. White
EGW	Ellen G. White
1888 Materials	*The Ellen G. White 1888 Materials* (4 vols.)
EW	*Early Writings*, by Ellen G. White
GCB	*General Conference Bulletin*
JL	Josiah Litch
JVH	Joshua V. Himes
JW	James White
LS	*Life Sketches of Ellen G. White* (1915 ed.)
LS (1888)	*Life Sketches of James and Ellen G. White* (1888 ed.)
MC	*Midnight Cry*
MS	Manuscript
MW	*Morning Watch*
PT	*Present Truth*
PUR	*Pacific Union Recorder*
RH	*Review and Herald*
SDA	Seventh-day Adventist
SG	*Spiritual Gifts*, by Ellen G. White (4 vols.)
SM	*Selected Messages*, by Ellen G. White (3 books)
ST	*Signs of the Times* (Millerite)
T	*Testimonies for the Church*, by Ellen G. White (9 vols.)
WCW	William C. White
WM	William Miller

A Word to the Reader

Seventh-day Adventists have never viewed themselves as just another denomination. To the contrary, from their beginning they have understood their movement to be a fulfillment of prophecy. Their role, as they have seen it, has been to preach the unique message of the three angels of Revelation 14:6-12, presenting God's last appeal to a dying world before Christ returns to "harvest" the earth (verses 14-20). Seventh-day Adventists eventually concluded that they needed to preach their special message "to every nation, and kindred, and tongue, and people" (verse 6). That belief, coupled with a sense of nearness of the end of earthly time, has impelled them into one of history's most energetic mission programs.

This book is the story of how Adventists came to view themselves as a prophetic people, of their growing awareness of a responsibility to take their unique message to all the world, and of their organizational and institutional development as they sought to fulfill their prophetic mission. The story, of course, is not complete. The mission goes forward even as you read these words.

The church and the world still look forward to the great climax of world history at the second coming of Jesus. Thus the history of Adventism stands incomplete. By the end of this volume, you as a reader and I as an author will find ourselves in the flow of Adventist history.

This book does not claim to be a "contribution to knowledge." Rather, it is largely a summary of the high points of Adventist history. In making that summary, however, this volume sets forth the material in a unique organizational format that should prove helpful to its readers as they seek to develop an understanding of the growth of the denomination.

I have written *A Brief History of Seventh-day Adventists* for those who seek a quick overview of Adventism's development. It will prove useful to church study groups, classroom students, new members, and others interested in the history of the denomination. The book seeks to develop the central lines of Adventist history, with a special interest in the growth of its concept of mission. While it does not seek to avoid significant problems in Adventism's past and present, it does suggest that our primary focus of concern should be on possibilities rather than problems.

As an Adventist historian, I am indebted to those who have gone before me. Most topics treated in this book are covered in more detail elsewhere. I have suggested additional readings for those who wish to pursue special lines of study.

Pacific Press published an earlier version of this volume in 1993 under the title *Anticipating the Advent*. The present revision represents an overall updating. That is especially true of the final chapter, which treats new issues and revises "old" statistics. Another major change is that I have added in-text references to the original sources for all direct quotations. Because of a lack of space, however, I have omitted the sources for general facts and indirect quotations.

It should be noted that *A Brief History of Seventh-day Adventists* could have done more with the secular and religious contexts in which Adventism arose, but the brevity of the treatment demanded that I keep contextual materials to a minimum.

The present book is intended to be the first of a series that highlights Seventh-day Adventist heritage. Other volumes in the series will include studies of the development of Adventist theology, church organization, lifestyle, education, and mission theory.

I should also point out that the Adventist Heritage Series is closely related to my series on Ellen White: *Meeting Ellen White: A Fresh Look at Her Life, Writings, and Major Themes* (1996); *Reading Ellen White: How to Understand and Apply Her Writings* (1997); *Ellen White's World: A Fascinating Look at the Times in Which She Lived* (1998); and *Walking With Ellen White: The Human Interest Story* (1999). It is my intention that the two series will provide both Adventists and those outside of the Adventist community with an overview of what Seventh-day Adventism "is all about." Each treatment is intended to be brief but accurate. While I have written each volume with an Adventist readership in mind, they are also aimed at presenting a solid introduction of their respective topics to the larger community.

I would like to express my appreciation to Jennifer Kharbteng and Joyce Werner, who entered the "handwriting" of my original manuscript into the computer; to Bonnie Beres, who rekeyed the revised manuscript in its entirety; to Robert W. Olson, Richard W. Schwarz, and Alberto R. Timm, who read the original manuscript and offered suggestions for its improvement; to Gerald Wheeler and Jeannette R. Johnson for shepherding the manuscript through the publication process; and to the administration of Andrews University for providing financial support and time for research and writing.

I trust that *A Brief History of Seventh-day Adventists* will be a blessing to its readers as they seek to learn more about Seventh-day Adventists and their history.

George R. Knight
Andrews University
Berrien Springs, Michigan

A Note on the Third Edition

The current edition updates denominational statistics and bibliography. Beyond that, it supplements the text in several places and makes a few factual corrections.

Since the publication of the first edition in 1999 I have added two volumes to the Adventist Heritage Series: *A Search for Identity: The Development of Seventh-day Adventist Beliefs* (2000) and *Organizing for Mission and Growth: The Development of Adventist Church Structure* (2006).

Appreciation is due to Kathleen A. Jones of the General Conference Office of Archives and Statistics for help in arriving at correct statistical estimates and to Cheryl D. Doss, director of the Institute of World Mission, for suggestions on updating the last chapter.

George R. Knight
July 12, 2012

CHAPTER 1

Millerite Roots

Modern Seventh-day Adventism finds its immediate roots in the Second Advent movement of the early nineteenth century. While many preachers proclaimed the soon coming of Christ in Europe and other parts of the world, the belief made its largest impact in North America. Central to North American Adventist beginnings was a Baptist layman by the name of William Miller (1782-1849).

William Miller: The Reluctant Prophet

Born into a Christian home, Miller abandoned his religious convictions for deism in the first years of the nineteenth century. Deism (a skeptical belief that rejects Christianity with its miracles and supernatural revelation) argues for a more distant God—one who does not actively participate in earthly affairs. Deistic beliefs became popular in both Europe and North America during the last half of the eighteenth century, but the atrocities and excesses of the French Revolution in the 1790s led many to question human reason as a sufficient basis for civilized living. One result was the widespread abandonment of deism and the return of many people to Christianity during the first two decades of the nineteenth century.

In the United States the ensuing revival became known as the Second Great Awakening. Miller was among those who returned to a belief in the Bible during the Awakening. His skepticism lasted through the War of 1812. But in the face of violence and death, he began to reevaluate his personal life and the meaning of life in general.

Like many of his generation, he felt impelled to study the Bible, and, also like many, he was converted or reconverted to Christianity as the Second Great Awakening revitalized the American churches. Unlike most of his contemporaries, though, Miller became an especially zealous Bible student.

His method of Bible study was to compare scripture with scripture in a methodical manner. "I commenced with Genesis," Miller wrote, "and read verse by verse, proceeding no faster than the meaning of the several passages should be so unfolded, as to leave me free from embarrassment. . . . Whenever I found any thing obscure, my practice was to compare it with all collateral passages; and by the help of CRUDEN ['s Bible concordance], I examined all the texts of Scripture in which were found any of the prominent words contained in any obscure portion. Then by letting every word have its proper bearing on the subject of the text, if my view of it harmonized with every collateral passage in the Bible, it ceased to be a difficulty" (A&D 6).

For two years (1816-1818) Miller studied his Bible intensively in this way. Finally he came to "the solemn conclusion . . . that in about twenty-five years from that time [i.e., 1843] all the affairs of our present state would be wound up" and Christ would come (*ibid.* 12).

Miller had reached his conclusion through a study of the prophecies of the book of Daniel, especially Daniel 8:14:

"Unto two thousand and three hundred days; then shall the sanctuary be cleansed." Operating on the commonly accepted understanding of Numbers 14:34 and Ezekiel 4:5, 6 that a day in prophecy equals a year, Miller calculated that the 2300-day prophecy would conclude in 1843. And, interpreting the sanctuary of Daniel 8:14 as the earth and its cleansing as the last-day purging of the earth by fire, Miller reasoned that Christ would return to the earth at the end of the 2300 days—about 1843. His heart filled with joy.

But he was also quite aware that his conclusion that Christ would return at the *beginning* of the millennium (1,000 years) of Revelation 20 flew in the face of the almost universally accepted theology of his day, which held that Christ would return at the *end* of the millennium. "I therefore," he penned, "feared to present it [his conclusion], lest by some possibility I should be in error, and be the means of misleading any" (*ibid.* 13).

Because of his fears, Miller spent another five years (1818-1823) reexamining his Bible and raising every objection he could to his conclusions. As a result he became more sure than ever that Christ would arrive about 1843. So after seven years he began to speak of his beliefs openly to his neighbors. However, he found only a "very few who listened with any interest" (*ibid.* 15).

For nine years (1823-1832) Miller continued to study his Bible. Meanwhile, he came increasingly under the conviction that he needed to share his findings of impending doom. The impression "'Go and tell the world of their danger'" continually assailed him. "I did all I could to avoid the conviction that any thing was required of me," Miller wrote. But he could not escape his conscience (*ibid.* 15, 16).

Miller finally "entered into a solemn covenant with God" that if God opened the way, he would do his duty. Feeling he needed to be more specific, Miller promised God that if he should receive an invitation to speak publicly in any place, he would go and teach about the Lord's second coming. "Instantly," he penned, "all my burden was gone; and I rejoiced that I should not probably be thus called upon; for I had never had such an invitation" (*ibid.* 17).

To Miller's dismay, however, within a half hour of his agreement with God he had his first request to preach on the Second Advent. "I was immediately angry with myself for having made the covenant," he confessed. "I rebelled at once against the Lord, and determined not to go." He then stomped out of his house to wrestle with the Lord in prayer, finally submitting after another hour (*ibid.* 18).

His first presentation on the Second Advent led to several conversions. Thereafter Miller had an unending stream of invitations to hold meetings in the churches of various denominations. By the end of the 1830s the reluctant prophet had won several ministers to his view that Christ would come about the year 1843. The most significant of those ministerial converts was Joshua V. Himes of the Christian Connexion.

Adventism Takes a Giant Step Forward With Joshua V. Himes

The year 1839 found Himes as the influential pastor of the Chardon Street Chapel in Boston. He was not only a prominent pastor but a recognized leader in the interchurch movement to bring about the earthly millennium through broad-based personal and social reform. In November 1839, however, Himes issued an invitation to William Miller to hold a series of meetings in his church. Miller's Second Advent message transformed the energetic Himes into the foremost publicist of his message—that Christ would return about the year 1843.

Sensing the urgency of the message, Himes felt a burden to

get the Advent doctrine before the world. He asked Miller why he had not preached in the large cities. Miller replied that he went only where invited. Such a passive approach was too much for the aggressive Himes, who inquired if Miller would go "where doors are opened." Miller replied in the affirmative. "I then told him," claimed Himes, that "he might prepare for the campaign; for doors should be opened in every city in the Union, and the warning should go to the ends of the earth! Here I began to 'help' Father Miller." Adventism was never the same after that (S. Bliss, *Memoirs of William Miller*, pp. 140, 141).

In the next four years the activist Himes made Millerism and Adventism household words in North America. Beyond North America, Himes's ingenuity saw to it that by 1844 the Advent doctrine had received a hearing around the world. He utilized several avenues to fulfill his mission of warning the globe that Christ would come about the year 1843 and that "*the hour of his judgment is come*" (Rev. 14:7). Perhaps the most important and influential was the printed page. Himes unleashed what historian Nathan Hatch has referred to as "an unprecedented media blitz" (*Democratization of American Christianity*, p. 142). Not being one to let any grass grow under his feet, within three months of his first invitation to Miller Himes had started publishing the *Signs of the Times* to get the Advent message before the world.

In addition to the *Signs*, in 1842 Himes began the *Midnight Cry* in an effort to wake up New York City to the nearness of Christ's return. He established the *Midnight Cry* as a two-cent daily newspaper in connection with a Millerite evangelistic campaign being held in the nation's metropolis. Himes had 10,000 copies printed daily for a number of weeks and either had them sold on the streets by newsboys or given away. At least one copy went to every minister in the state of New York. In 1842 alone he distributed more than 600,000 copies of the

Midnight Cry in five months. When the New York campaign closed, the paper became a weekly.

Himes's exploits in periodical publication soon stimulated imitators, and Adventist literature began coming off the press with unprecedented urgency.

Beyond periodicals, Himes also guided the publication of a vast array of pamphlets, tracts, and books. Many of them were collected into the Second Advent Library, which people could purchase for under $10 to circulate in local communities. By July 1841 the Adventist publishing program had grown to such an extent that it had to employ Josiah Litch (a Methodist minister) to serve as "general agent" for the Committee of Publication. That arrangement left Himes free to respond to calls for travel and preaching in behalf of Millerite publications.

Meanwhile, he was not content with spreading the Advent message through publications alone. A born organizer, the dynamic Himes initiated the first General Conference of Christians Expecting the Advent in October 1840. That Boston "general conference" led to at least 15 more before 1844, along with scores of local Millerite conferences.

More important, however, Himes also had a forceful role in developing the Adventist camp meeting. Beginning in the summer of 1842 the Millerites held more than 130 camp meetings before the autumn of 1844. It is estimated that their combined attendance exceeded 500,000 (approximately one out of every 35 Americans). The impact of the camp meetings, however, affected many more than just those attending, since media blitzes accompanied them and they were held in or near large cities.

To accommodate the camp meeting crowds in locales where outside meetings were inappropriate and proper buildings were unavailable, Himes pioneered in the use of a tent. With a seating capacity of approximately 4,000, the Millerite tent was apparently the largest of its kind in the United States up through that time. The novelty of the big tent, of course, also attracted listeners. It is reported that in some locations several thousand people, unable to get into the tent, stood listening on the outside.

Many parts of the world outside of North America also heard the Millerite message. The Millerite method for worldwide outreach was generally not to send missionaries, but to place their publications on ships bound to various seaports. Thus by the summer of 1842 Himes could write that Millerite publications had been "sent to all the Missionary stations that we know of on the globe" (ST, Aug. 3, 1842). Under his guidance the Advent message made a significant impact in North America and was at least "heard" through the printed word in other parts of the world. That success, however, met with resistance among the churches as the inevitable reaction set in.

Charles Fitch and the "Fall of Babylon"

The Millerite preaching that Christ would return about the year 1843 directly contradicted the generally accepted Protestant teaching that Christ would come after the millennium. While the pulpits and church buildings of most denominations had been opened to Adventist preachers during the early 1840s, things began to change in 1843. Millerites came under progressively more ridicule and often had to decide between their Advent belief and that of their denominations. Those choosing to retain their faith in the soon return of Christ increasingly found themselves disfellowshipped by their congregations. In other words, as the "year of the end" approached, a confrontation between theologies of the Second Advent flared up.

In that context Charles Fitch (a popular Millerite minister of the Congregationalist denomination) preached a sermon on

Revelation 18 in the summer of 1843 focusing on the fall of Babylon. "Come out of her, my people" (Rev. 18:2, 4; cf. 14:8) was his message. That sermon, later published in both article and tract form, signaled another shift in Millerite development as the Advent believers progressively came to view themselves as a separate body.

Up through the summer of 1843 the Millerites, in harmony with most Protestants, had generally identified the Papacy as the Babylon of Revelation 18:1-5. But, argued Fitch, Babylon is antichrist, and anyone who opposes the personal reign of Jesus Christ over this world is antichrist. Fitch's definition of the antichrist included all Catholics and Protestants who rejected the teaching of a soon-coming Christ.

"To come out of Babylon," Fitch wrote, "is to be converted to the true scriptural doctrine of the personal coming and kingdom of Christ. . . . If you are a Christian, *come out of Babylon!* If you intend to be found a Christian when Christ appears, *come out of Babylon*, and come out Now! . . . Come out of Babylon or perish" (*Come Out of Her, My People*, pp. 18, 19, 24). Thus Fitch provided many Millerite Adventists with a theological rationale for separating into a distinct body before the close of earth's probation. The call was to leave those churches that had rejected the judgment-hour message.

While most Eastern Millerite leaders initially responded coolly to Fitch's call for separation, the aggressive reaction within the various denominations made it acceptable to many Advent believers as they faced increasing opposition and loss of membership. Himes did not become an advocate of separation until the autumn of 1844, and then only reluctantly. Miller never could bring himself to urge separation, even though the Low Hampton Baptist Church, where he was a member, eventually expelled him.

In the end, separation was not a choice but something impelled by the force of events as the world entered the predicted "year of the end."

The Passing of the Time

Miller originally had resisted being too specific about the exact time of Christ's return. His message emphasized "about the year 1843." But by January 1843 he had come to the conclusion, on the basis of the 2300-day prophecy of Daniel 8:14 and the Jewish calendar, that Christ would return sometime between March 21, 1843, and March 21, 1844. "PREPARE TO MEET THY GOD," headlined the *Western Midnight Cry* of March 8, 1844, as the end of that period approached. But, needless to say, Miller's "year of the end of the world" passed without the return of Christ. Thus the Millerites experienced their first disappointment.

A frustrated but deeply sincere William Miller wrote to Himes on March 25, 1844: "I am now seated at my old desk. . . . Having obtained help of God until the present time, I am still looking for the dear Saviour. . . . The time, as I have calculated it, is now filled up; and I expect every moment to see the Saviour descend from heaven. . . . Whether God designs for me to warn the people of this earth any more, or not, I am at a loss to know. . . . I hope I have cleansed my garments from the blood of souls. I feel that as far as it was in my power, I have freed myself from all guilt in their condemnation" (MC, Apr. 18, 1844).

An equally frustrated Himes editorialized on April 24, 1844: "In the passing by of the Jewish year, our friends and the public . . . have a right to expect from us some exposition of the position we occupy. . . . We . . . fully and frankly admit that all our expected and published time . . . has passed: the Jewish year . . . has expired, and the Savior has not been revealed; and we would not disguise the fact at all, that we were *mistaken* in the precise time of the termination of the prophetic periods."

Yet, Himes significantly added, "We have never been able to find any other time for the termination of the prophetic periods." He then went on to build hope in his readers by noting that "we are placed in a position, which God foresaw his children would be placed in, at the end of the vision; and for which he made provision, by the prophet Habakkuk."

After all, did not the prophet write: "For the vision is yet for an appointed time, but at the end it shall speak, and not lie: *though it tarry, wait for it; because it will surely come*" (Hab. 2:3). Himes connected that text with Matthew 25:5, which points out that the bridegroom delays before he comes, while those waiting "slumbered and slept."

On the basis of those texts, Himes could say that "we are now prepared to tell the world what we shall do. . . . We intend to hold fast the integrity of our faith without wavering. . . . We shall continue to believe God's word, in its literal acceptation: for not one jot or tittle of all that is written therein will fail" (AH, Apr. 24, 1844).

Thus the Millerite Adventists entered the "tarrying time." Their movement had been saved from disintegration by the fact that it had had some imprecision regarding the exact date for the prophetic fulfillment and by the application of Habakkuk's prophecy and other texts to its situation. The Adventists had been disappointed, but the movement went on, albeit with less enthusiasm than before.

The Seventh-Month Movement and the "True Midnight Cry"

Millerism found a new lease on life at the Exeter, New Hampshire, camp meeting in mid-August 1844. At that convocation, Millerite minister S. S. Snow convincingly demonstrated through a variety of mathematical calculations that the fulfillment of the 2300-day prophecy of Daniel 8:14 would take place in the autumn of 1844. In fact, through extensive study of the ceremonies of the Jewish year, Snow predicted that Daniel's prophecy about the cleansing of the sanctuary would meet its completion on the Jewish Day of Atonement—the tenth day of the seventh month of the Jewish year (see Lev. 23:27).

Snow claimed that he had calculated the exact day for the cleansing, which the Millerites still universally interpreted as the second coming of Christ. That day in 1844, according to Karaite Jewish reckoning, was October 22. Thus Christ would return, Snow said, on October 22, 1844—in about two months.

The idea electrified his audience. They left the Exeter meeting to spread their urgent message as quickly and as widely as possible. "Behold," they proclaimed, "the Bridegroom cometh!" Christ is coming on the tenth day of the seventh month! Time is short; get ready! Get ready! Although Miller, Himes, and other leading Adventists hesitated to fix their hopes on a definite day, the seventh-month enthusiasm spread like fire in stubble among the bulk of the believers.

The words of George Storrs give us a feel for the epidemic enthusiasm. In September he wrote, "I take up my pen with feelings such as I never before experienced. *Beyond a doubt*, in my mind, the *tenth day* of the *seventh month*, will witness the revelation of our Lord Jesus Christ in the clouds of heaven. We are then within a *few days* of that event. Awful moment to those who are unprepared—but glorious to those who are ready. I feel that I am making the *last* appeal that I shall ever make through the press. My heart is full. . . . Alas! we have all been *slumbering and sleeping*—both the *wise* and the *foolish*; but so our Saviour told us it would be; and 'thus the Scriptures are fulfilled,' and it is the last prophecy relating to the events to precede the *personal advent* of our Lord; now comes the TRUE *Midnight Cry*. The previous was but the *alarm*. NOW THE REAL ONE IS SOUNDING: and oh, how solemn the hour" (MC, Oct. 3, 1844).

Miller, Himes, and other Millerite leaders eventually capitulated to the forcefulness of Snow's arguments. On October 6, 1844, Miller wrote of his enthusiasm and hopes: "Dear Bro. Himes:—I see a glory in the seventh month which I never saw before. . . . Thank the Lord, O my soul. Let Brother Snow, Brother Storrs and others be blessed for their instrumentality in opening my eyes. *I am almost home, Glory! Glory!! Glory!!! I see that the time is correct. . . .*

"My *soul is so full I cannot write.* I call on you, and all who love his appearing, to thank him for this glorious truth. My *doubts, and fears, and darkness, are all gone. I see that we are yet right. God's word is true; and my soul is full of joy. . . .* Oh, how I wish I could shout. But I will shout when the 'King of kings comes.'

"Methinks I hear you say, 'Bro. Miller is now a fanatic.' Very well, call me what you please; I care not; Christ will come in the seventh month, and will bless us all. Oh! glorious hope" (MC, Oct. 12, 1844; italics supplied).

On October 16 Himes announced that the *Advent Herald* (previously *Signs of the Times*) would cease publication. "As the date of the present number of the *Herald* is our last day of publication before the tenth day of the seventh month, we shall make no provision for issuing a paper for the week following. . . . We are shut up to this faith; . . . Behold, the Bridegroom cometh; go ye out to meet him!" (AH, Oct. 16, 1844).

At this distance we can only imagine the excitement in the Millerite ranks, but we can capture some of it if we ask ourselves, How would I feel if I *knew* Christ was coming in a few short days? How would I act? How would I order my priorities?

In their conviction and exuberance, the believers put their all into a final effort to warn the world of its impending doom. They made no provision for the future—they didn't need to. Some left their crops unharvested, closed their shops, and resigned from their jobs. Jesus was coming. The thought was like honey in the mouth, but unbeknown to them, it would be bitter in the belly (see Rev. 10:8-10).

The "Great Disappointment"

On October 22 tens of thousands of believers lingered in expectation of the appearance of Jesus in the clouds, while countless others waited in doubt, fearing that the Millerites might be correct. But the day came and went, thus encouraging the scoffers and fearful, but leaving the Millerites in total disarray and discouragement. Their specific claims about the time and their unbounded confidence in the October 22 date served to heighten their disappointment.

On October 24 Josiah Litch wrote to Miller: "It is a cloudy and dark day here—the sheep are scattered—and the Lord has not come yet" (JL to WM and JVH, Oct. 24, 1844).

Hiram Edson later penned: "Our fondest hopes and expectations were blasted, and such a spirit of weeping came over us as I never experienced before. It seemed that the loss of all earthly friends could have been no comparison. We wept, and wept, till the day dawn" (H. Edson MS).

And Washington Morse mused, "That day came and passed, and the darkness of another night closed in upon the world. *But with that darkness came a pang of disappointment to the Advent believers that can find a parallel only in the sorrow of the disciples after the crucifixion of their Lord.* The passing of the time was a bitter disappointment. True believers had given up all for Christ, and had shared His presence as never before. The love of Jesus filled every soul; and with inexpressible desire they prayed, 'Come, Lord Jesus, and come quickly;' but He did not come. *And now, to turn again to the cares, perplexities, and dangers of life, in full view of jeering and reviling unbelievers who scoffed as never before, was a terrible trial of faith and patience.* When Elder Himes visited Waterbury, Vt., a short time after the passing of the time, and stated that the brethren should prepare for another cold winter, my feelings were almost uncontrollable. I left the place of meeting and wept like a child" (RH, May 7, 1901; italics supplied).

We might expect Miller, as founder and titular head of the movement, to be terribly shaken by the experience. On the surface, however, he maintained an upbeat public-relations stance. "Although I have been twice disappointed," he stated on November 10, 1844, "I am not yet cast down or discouraged. God has been with me in Spirit, and has comforted me. . . . Although surrounded with enemies and scoffers, yet my mind is perfectly calm, and my hope in the coming of Christ is as strong as ever. I have done only what after years of sober consideration I felt to be my solemn duty. . . .

"*Brethren*, hold fast; let no man take your crown. I have fixed my mind upon another time, and here I mean to stand until God gives me more light.—And that is *To-day*, TO-DAY, and TO-DAY, until He comes, and I see Him for whom my soul yearns" (MC, Dec. 5, 1844).

In spite of those reassuring words, the bulk of the Millerites probably gave up their Second Advent faith. Meanwhile, those who continued to hope for the soon coming of Christ saw their once fairly harmonious movement dissolve into chaos as different leaders and self-appointed "leaders" put forth conflicting claims and counterclaims regarding the meaning of their experience and the "truth" about the Second Advent.

Out of that seething cauldron and shapeless mass of discouragement and confusion would come the Seventh-day Adventist Church. But, of course, no one could have predicted that development in 1844. That story will be the focus of our next two chapters.

For Those Who Would Like to Read More

Froom, LeRoy Edwin. *The Prophetic Faith of Our Fathers*. Washington, D.C.: Review and Herald, 1954. Vol. 4, pp. 443-851.

Gordon, Paul A. *Herald of the Midnight Cry*. Boise, Idaho: Pacific Press, 1990.

Knight, George R. *A Search for Identity: The Development of Seventh-day Adventist Beliefs*. Hagerstown, Md.: Review and Herald, 2000. Pp. 38-54.

———. *William Miller and the Rise of Adventism*. Nampa, Idaho: Pacific Press, 2010.

———, ed. *1844 and the Rise of Sabbatarian Adventism*. Hagerstown, Md.: Review and Herald, 1994. Pp. 1-142. (This volume contains reproductions of most of the documents cited in this chapter.)

Land, Gary, ed. *Adventism in America: A History*, rev. ed. Berrien Springs, Mich.: Andrews University Press, 1998. Pp. 1-28.

Maxwell, C. Mervyn. *Tell It to the World: The Story of Seventh-day Adventists*. 2nd rev. ed. Mountain View, Calif.: Pacific Press, 1977. Pp. 9-33.

Neufeld, Don F., ed. *The Seventh-day Adventist Encyclopedia*, 2nd rev. ed. Hagerstown, Md.: Review and Herald, 1996. Vol. 2, pp. 73-82.

Nichol, Francis D. *The Midnight Cry*. Washington, D.C.: Review and Herald, 1944.

Schwarz, Richard W., and Floyd Greenleaf. *Light Bearers: A History of the Seventh-day Adventist Church*. Nampa, Idaho: Pacific Press, 2000. Pp. 13-50.

CHAPTER 2

Era of Doctrinal Development

(1844-1848)

The aftermath of the great disappointment of October 22, 1844, found Millerite Adventism in a state of utter confusion. The height of their hope had led to the depth of their despair. The mathematical certainty of their faith left them in shock when the expected event failed to take place. It is impossible to get a completely accurate picture of the disappointed Millerites, but it is probable that the majority abandoned their Advent faith and either went back to their previous churches or drifted into secular unbelief.

We can roughly view those who maintained their hope in the soon return of Christ as belonging to one of three groups, depending upon their interpretation of what had occurred on October 22. The most easily identifiable group, under the leadership of Joshua V. Himes, rapidly came to believe that *nothing had happened on that date*.

Holding that they had been correct as to the expected event (that is, the second coming of Christ), they concluded that they had been wrong on the time calculation. On November 5, 1844, Himes wrote that "we are now satisfied that the authorities on which we based our calculations cannot be depended upon for *definite time*." Although "we are near the end, . . . we have no knowledge of a *fixed date* or *definite time*, but do most fully believe that we should watch and wait for the coming of Christ, as an event that may take place at any hour" (MC, Nov. 7, 1844; italics supplied).

Under Himes's leadership this group took steps to organize itself into a distinct Adventist body at Albany, New York, in April 1845. The aging William Miller, under Himes's influence, lent his authority to the Albany movement. One reason for the move to organize was that fanaticism ran rampant throughout the Adventist ranks. Thus we should see the Albany Conference as an attempt at stabilization.

That brings us to a second identifiable group of post-Disappointment Adventists—the "spiritualizers." This sector of Adventism got its name from the fact that it offered a spiritual interpretation to the event of October 22. The spiritualizers held that both the time and the event had been correct. In other words, *Christ had returned on October 22*, but it had been a spiritual coming.

Fanaticism easily arose among the spiritualizers. Some claimed to be sinless, while others refused to work, since they were in the millennial Sabbath. Still others, following the biblical injunction that they should become as little children, discarded forks and knives and crawled around on their hands and knees. Needless to say, outbreaks of charismatic enthusiasm swept through their midst.

A third strain of post-Disappointment Adventism appears among those who claimed that they had been correct on the time but wrong in the expected event. In other words, *something did happen on October 22, but it was not the Second Advent.* Among them were the future leaders of what would eventually develop into Seventh-day Adventism.

To this group it seemed that the majority party under Himes had abandoned the Adventist message by denying the validity of their experience in the 1844 movement. Although originally the smallest of the groups, it came to see itself as the true successor of the once-powerful Millerite movement.

Of the three divisions of Millerism discussed above, the third one was the last to gain visibility. Even before it could be defined as a distinct form of Adventism, it had to explain two things: (1) What *did* happen on October 22, 1844? and (2) What was the sanctuary that needed to be cleansed?

Redefining the Sanctuary

The first step toward a clearer understanding of the above questions took place on October 23, 1844. On that day Hiram Edson, a Methodist farmer of Port Gibson, New York, became convicted during a session of prayer with fellow believers "that light should be given" and our "disappointment be explained." Soon thereafter he and a companion set out to encourage their fellow believers. As they crossed a field, Edson reported, "I was stopped about midway" and "heaven seemed open to my view. . . . I saw distinctly, and clearly, that instead of our High Priest coming out of the Most Holy of the heavenly sanctuary to come to this earth on the tenth day of the seventh month, at the end of the 2300 days, that he for the first time entered on that day the second apartment of that sanctuary; and that he had a work to perform in the Most Holy before coming to this earth."

Edson's mind was also "directed" to Revelation 10, with its account of the little book that was sweet in the mouth but bitter in the stomach. Identifying the Millerites' experience in preaching on the prophecies of Daniel as the bittersweet experience of Revelation 10, Edson noted that the chapter closed with the command to "prophesy again."

At that point the call of his companion, who had gone on ahead of him, brought Edson's awareness back to his surroundings. When asked what was wrong, Edson replied that "the Lord was answering our morning prayer; by giving light with regard to our disappointment."

Edson's "vision" soon led him into extended Bible study with O.R.L. Crosier and Dr. F. B. Hahn. They concluded, in line with Edson's October 23 experience, that the sanctuary to be cleansed in Daniel 8:14 was not the earth or the church, but the sanctuary in heaven, of which the earthly sanctuary had been a type or copy.

Hahn and Edson decided that their discoveries were "just what the scattered remnant needed" to explain the Disappointment and "set the brethren on the right track." As a result they agreed to share publishing expenses if Crosier would "write out the subject of the sanctuary." According to Edson, Crosier began to print the findings of their combined study in the *Day-Dawn* during early 1845 (H. Edson MS).

Then, on February 7, 1846, Enoch Jacobs published their findings in the *Day-Star Extra* under the title "The Law of Moses." By that time their position had fairly well matured. Through Bible study, Crosier and his colleagues had provided answers to the questions of What happened on October 22, 1844? and What was the sanctuary that needed to be cleansed?

We can summarize their most important conclusions, as presented in "The Law of Moses," as follows: 1. A literal sanctuary exists in heaven. 2. The Hebrew sanctuary system was a complete visual representation of the plan of salvation that was *patterned after the heavenly sanctuary*. 3. Just as the earthly priests had a two-phase ministry in the wilderness sanctuary, so Christ has a two-phase ministry in the heavenly. The first phase began in the holy place at His ascension, while the second started on October 22, 1844, when Christ moved from the first apartment of the heavenly sanctuary to the second. Thus the antitypical or heavenly day of atonement commenced on that date. 4. The first phase of Christ's ministry dealt with forgiveness; the second involves the blotting out of sins and the cleansing of both the sanctuary and individual believers. 5. The cleansing of Daniel 8:14 was a cleansing from sin and therefore accomplished by blood rather than fire. 6. Christ would not return to earth until He completed His second apartment ministry.

Thus the combined study of Edson, Crosier, and Hahn confirmed Edson's October 23 "vision." By intensive study of such books as Hebrews and Leviticus in connection with Daniel 7 through 9 and the book of Revelation, they had arrived at an explanation of both the cleansing and the sanctuary that needed it. They had also begun to understand faintly the command of Revelation 10:11 that the disappointed ones "must prophesy again before many peoples, and nations, and tongues, and kings." However, during the late 1840s, as we shall see, their idea of prophesying to the world involved preaching their newfound truth only to those Millerites who had not yet seen the light on "the cleansing of the sanctuary" and related doctrines.

The new understanding of the cleansing of the sanctuary became a primary building block in the development of what would become Seventh-day Adventist theology. Coupled with the belief in the soon return of Christ inherited from Miller, the two-phase heavenly ministry of Christ became a foundational teaching for what grew into a denomination during the next two decades.

Before moving away from the cleansing of the sanctuary, we should note that Adventists soon linked this teaching to the idea of the investigative or pre-Advent judgment.

Miller, of course, had tied the judgment scene of Daniel 7,

the cleansing of the sanctuary of Daniel 8:14, and "the hour of his judgment is come" of Revelation 14:7 to the judgment to take place at the Second Advent. However, as early as 1840 one of Miller's chief lieutenants had taught the necessity of a pre-Advent judgment. In February of that year Methodist preacher Josiah Litch indicated that the judgment must take place *before* the resurrection. By 1842 Litch had refined his view and pointed out that the divine acts of raising some persons to life while putting others to death at the Second Coming constitute an executive judgment that must of necessity have a preliminary "trial" judgment (*Prophetic Expositions*, vol. 1, pp. 49-54). The group evolving into Seventh-day Adventists would later develop that theme. Crosier, while not making the pre-Advent judgment explicit in his February 1846 article, pointed out that the high priest did wear the breastplate of judgment on the Day of Atonement and that the cleansing of the sanctuary was a purging from sin.

It was only a short step beyond that position for Joseph Bates (an ex-sea captain and an active Millerite layman) in 1847, and others as early as 1845, to equate the heavenly day of atonement with a pre-Advent judgment that must of necessity occur before Christ could return to execute the Advent judgment, at which all would then receive their just rewards. Although resisted at first by some (including James White, a young preacher of the Christian Connexion, who had become a forceful advocate of the 1844 message), that teaching became firmly entrenched by the mid-1850s.

Thus the developing Seventh-day Adventist theology came to see the cleansing of the sanctuary of Daniel 8:14 as Christ's act of investigative or pre-Advent judgment in the Most Holy Place of the heavenly sanctuary. As a result, when those evolving into Seventh-day Adventists preached the first angel's message ("the hour of his judgment is come" [Rev. 14:7]), they eventually interpreted it as an announcement of the beginning of the pre-Advent judgment on October 22, 1844.

So far we have examined the development of two distinctive pillars of what was becoming Seventh-day Adventist theology: (1) the personal, soon-coming, premillennial return of Jesus—a belief inherited from the Millerites; and (2) the two-apartment ministry of Christ, including the pre-Advent judgment—a doctrinal position that believers came to understand as they struggled with the meaning of the cleansing of the sanctuary in Daniel 8:14.

Thus while the majority of the Millerite Adventists, under the leadership of Himes, looked back on the time element in their interpretation of the 2300-day prophecy of Daniel 8:14 as an error, the group evolving into Seventh-day Adventism held that the Millerites had been correct on the time, but wrong as to the event to take place on October 22, 1844. After all, they noted, no one had been able to refute Miller's time calculations. But further study made it obvious to them that the Millerites had misinterpreted the symbolism of both the "cleansing" and the "sanctuary."

This small band of struggling believers refused to step off the prophetic platform that had made the Millerite movement such a powerful force. Rather, while building on Miller's and Snow's insights, they made what they believed to be necessary corrections to them. They felt deeply convicted that God had called Miller to enlighten the world with the message of the nearness of the Second Advent.

The Gift of Prophecy

Intimately related to the prophetic validity of the Millerite message and the correctness of the October 22 date was the call of 17-year-old Ellen Harmon (Ellen White after her marriage in 1846) to the prophetic ministry. Along with most other

Millerites, in November 1844 she gave up her faith that anything had happened on October 22. But to her surprise, she later recalled, "while I was praying at the family altar [in December 1844], the Holy Ghost fell upon me." In vision, when she looked for her fellow Adventists and could not see them, a voice told her to look a little higher. "At this," she recounted, "I raised my eyes, and saw a straight and narrow path. . . . On this path the Advent people were traveling to the [heavenly] city, which was at the farther end of the path. They had a bright light set up behind them at the beginning of the path, which an angel told me was the midnight cry." In this way God confirmed that the October 22 date was a fulfillment of prophecy.

"This light," Ellen Harmon continued, "shone all along the path and gave light for their [the saints'] feet so that they might not stumble. If they kept their eyes fixed on Jesus, who was just before them, leading them to the city, they were safe."

But some, she reported, "rashly denied the light behind them and said that it was not God that had led them out so far." For them, "the light behind them went out, leaving their feet in perfect darkness," and they "fell off the path down into the dark and wicked world below" (EW 14, 15).

Her first vision tells us a great deal about Ellen Harmon's ministry. First and foremost it points us to her lifelong passion—the soon return of Jesus and God's care for His children. Beyond that, it presents a dual emphasis that runs throughout her 70-year ministry.

The first aspect of that emphasis is that something of great importance took place in heaven on October 22, 1844, and that Adventists should never forget their place in prophetic history. Thus she could later write that "we have nothing to fear for the future, except as we shall forget the way the Lord has led us, and His teaching in our past history." Adventists, she held, are a prophetic people (LS 196).

The second aspect of her dual emphasis was that individuals must keep their eyes focused on Jesus, their Savior. Thus Adventists are not only a distinctively prophetic people; they are also a Christian people. As we shall see in chapter 5, she greatly emphasized this second aspect of her dual focus during the post-1888 period as she sought to get Adventism to bring the two aspects of its belief system into proper perspective.

For 70 years (from 1844 through her death in 1915) Ellen White preached God's love, the nearness of Christ's coming, and God's judgment-hour message. At the beginning, of course, she had little authority. Most believers perceived her as just one voice among many. But gradually the members of the developing denomination began to recognize her prophetic message as a communication from God to guide His people through the crisis of the end-times.

Not surprisingly, given the charismatic fanaticism evident in some sectors of post-1844 Adventism, she did not want to be God's spokesperson. She was also undoubtedly aware that Millerism, because of some sad experiences, had a deep prejudice against visions and private revelations. In fact, in May 1845 the Albany group went on record as having "no confidence in any new messages, visions, dreams, tongues, miracles, extraordinary gifts, revelations," and so on (MW, May 5, 1845). It has never been easy to be God's prophet, and that was certainly true in 1844—the very year that Joseph Smith, the Mormon "prophet," lost his life to a mob in Illinois. But God told Ellen Harmon that He would strengthen her. As time passed, Adventists increasingly felt impressed with the soundness of her message. By applying the biblical tests of a prophet to her life and work, more and more people confirmed their belief in her call.

At this juncture we should point out that Ellen Harmon was not God's first or only choice for the prophetic office among Adventists. Early in 1842 William Foy, a Black freedman belonging to the Baptist Church, received a number of visions dealing with the second coming of Christ and the reward of the righteous. Foy preached his messages for some time. Then, shortly before the Great Disappointment, God called a second man, Hazen Foss, to the prophetic office, but he refused to cooperate and lost the gift. Foss later encouraged Ellen Harmon not to make the same mistake.

Before moving away from this section on the gift of prophecy, we should note that Ellen White's gift did not play a prominent role in the development of Adventist doctrine. In an 1874 response to critics who claimed that Seventh-day Adventists had received their sanctuary doctrine through the visions of Ellen White, the denomination's leading editor replied: "Hundreds of articles have been written upon the subject. But in no one of these are the visions once referred to as any authority on this subject, or the source from whence any view we hold has been derived. . . . The appeal is invariably to the Bible, where there is abundant evidence for the views we hold on this subject" (RH, Dec. 22, 1874).

The same could be said for each of the great doctrinal positions of Adventism. The primary method used by the pioneers in their doctrinal formation was to study the Bible until a general consensus developed. At that point Ellen White would sometimes receive a vision on a topic already studied, primarily to reaffirm the consensus and to help those who were still out of harmony with the majority to accept the correctness of the group's biblically derived conclusions. Thus we can best view Mrs. White's role in doctrinal development as confirmation rather than initiation. As we shall see in chapter 4, however, she sometimes played a more prominent role in the development of positions in the area of Adventist lifestyle than she did in doctrinal formation.

Some early Adventist leaders were quite sensitive to a possible misuse of the gift of prophecy. For example, for years Adventists differed with each other over the exact time to begin and close the Sabbath. After a thorough study of the Bible, a consensus emerged in 1855 that the Sabbath began and ended at sunset. Bates, however, still held out for the 6:00 position. At that point Mrs. White received a vision confirming the sunset-to-sunset view already established through a study of the Bible. That was enough to bring Bates and his colleagues into harmony with the others. Interestingly enough, that vision also changed Ellen White's view on the topic.

The question then arose as to why God didn't just settle issues by providing visions in the first place. James White's reply provides us with a crucial understanding of the role of his wife's gift. "*It does not appear,*" he penned, "*to be the desire of the Lord to teach his people by the gifts of the Spirit on the Bible questions until his servants have diligently searched his word. . . . Let the gifts have their proper place in the church. God has never set them in the very front,* and commanded us to look to them to lead us in the path of truth, and the way to Heaven. *His word he has magnified.* The Scriptures of the Old and New Testament are man's lamp to light up his path to the kingdom. Follow that. But if you err from Bible truth, and are in danger of being lost, it may be that God will in the time of his choice correct you, and bring you back to the Bible, and save you" (RH, Feb. 25, 1868; italics supplied).

Seventh-day Adventism at its best has been a Bible-oriented movement that accepts the scriptural teaching of the gift of prophecy. However, one of the unfortunate aspects of Adventist history is that some church members have too often abused Ellen White's gift by giving it more prominence than the Bible. Both of the Whites and the other founders of Adventism rejected that nonbiblical position. The gift of prophecy is a blessing to God's church, but true Adventism has always uplifted the primacy of Scripture.

The Sabbath

Simultaneously with the above doctrinal developments, those Adventists holding to the heavenly sanctuary teaching and the validity of the October 22 date began to gain a fuller understanding of the law of God and the seventh-day Sabbath.

The first Adventists to accept the seventh-day Sabbath heard of it from the Seventh Day Baptists, who in the early 1840s had renewed their burden to spread their special insight. One of their members, an aggressive woman named Rachel Oakes, challenged an Adventist preacher belonging to the Methodist Church to keep *all* of God's commandments. As a result, Pastor Frederick Wheeler began to observe the seventh day in the spring of 1844.

About that same time several members of the Washington, New Hampshire, church, where Wheeler often preached, also began worshiping on the biblical Sabbath. Thus the first Sabbathkeeping Adventist congregation came into being before the Great Disappointment.

In the summer of 1844 T. M. Preble, a Free Will Baptist preacher who had become a Millerite, also accepted the Sabbath through his contacts with the Washington congregation. Realizing that time was short, neither Wheeler nor Preble felt a burden to make an issue of their newfound Sabbath message.

After the Great Disappointment, however, Preble published his Sabbath beliefs in the February 28, 1845, issue of the *Hope of Israel*. Later that year he again set forth his views in a 12-page pamphlet with the not-so-subtle title *Tract, Showing That the Seventh Day Should Be Observed as the Sabbath, Instead of the First Day; "According to the Commandment."*

In March of 1845 Preble's writings fell into the hands of

Joseph Bates, one of the three primary founders of the Seventh-day Adventist Church. Bates accepted the Sabbath, and in August 1846 the ex-sea captain published a tract entitled *The Seventh Day Sabbath, a Perpetual Sign.* That little volume led James and Ellen Harmon (who married on August 30, 1846) to the seventh-day Sabbath. Years later Ellen White remembered that "in the autumn of 1846 we began to observe the Bible Sabbath, and to teach and defend it" (1T 75). Thus the three founders of Seventh-day Adventism had united on the Sabbath doctrine by the end of 1846.

By that time Bates also had shared the Bible's teaching on the Sabbath with Crosier, Hahn, and Edson. All three initially accepted it, but Crosier and Hahn eventually reverted back to Sundaykeeping. Meanwhile, Bates and the Whites had adopted their insights on the heavenly sanctuary. Thus by late 1846 a small group of Adventist believers began to form around the united doctrines of the ministry of Christ in the heavenly sanctuary and the binding nature of the seventh-day Sabbath. From this point on in our discussion we will refer to them as Sabbatarian Adventists. They formed the nucleus of what, in the early 1860s, became the Seventh-day Adventist Church.

Bates gave to the seventh-day Sabbath a richness and prophetic meaning that it never could have had among the Seventh Day Baptists. For the Baptists the seventh day was merely the correct day. But with Bates, steeped as he was in a prophetic faith informed by extensive study of the books of Daniel and the Revelation, the seventh-day Sabbath took on an eschatological (end-time) richness that went beyond the realm of Baptist understanding.

Through a series of small books Bates interpreted the Sabbath within the framework of Revelation 11-14. Between 1846 and 1849 he made at least three contributions to a prophetic understanding of the Sabbath. First, he began to see connections between the Sabbath and the sanctuary. As he studied the sounding of the seventh trumpet in Revelation 11:15-19 (a passage obviously having to do with the last days), Bates felt himself particularly drawn to verse 19: "And the temple of God was opened in heaven, and there was seen in his temple the ark of his testament."

Bates noted a recent upsurge of writing on the seventh-day Sabbath. Why? When the seventh angel began to sound, he proposed, the second apartment of the temple of God opened in heaven and the ark of the covenant was spiritually revealed and people began to search the Scriptures. The ark of the covenant in the earthly sanctuary, of course, contained the Ten Commandments. Thus, through typological comparison, he concluded that the Most Holy Place of the heavenly sanctuary had an ark containing the Decalogue, as did the earthly sanctuary. God's law eventually came to be seen as the basis for the pre-Advent judgment that had been under way since October 22, 1844. On that date the second apartment had opened in heaven, exposing the ark of the covenant and pointing to a renewed emphasis on God's law.

Bates's second contribution to the developing understanding of the Sabbath in prophetic history came through his study of the three angels' messages of Revelation 14. He presented them as sequential. The first two (the hour of God's judgment and the fall of Babylon), he said, the Millerites had preached. But he held that verse 12, "Here is the patience of the saints: here are they that *keep the commandments of God,*" began to be fulfilled after October 22, 1844. Thus, he wrote in 1847, a people "have been uniting in companies for the last two years, on the commandments of God" (*Seventh-day Sabbath* [1847 ed.], p. 59).

Bates, of course, did not lose the prophetic forcefulness of

Revelation 12:17: "And the dragon was wroth with the woman, and went to make war with the remnant of her seed, which keep [all] the commandments of God." That "war," he held, Revelation 13 described as the beast powers seeking to overcome God's commandment-keeping people, finally issuing the death decree of verse 15. Thus Bates's third contribution to Sabbath theology (in the framework of prophecy) was to develop the end-time concepts of the seal of God and the mark of the beast in the context of allegiance either to God or to the beast. Faithfulness to the biblical Sabbath, he held, would be the outward focal point in the struggle.

Conditional Immortality

The final distinctive Adventist doctrine is that of conditional immortality. Most Christians throughout history have believed, following Greek philosophy, that people are born immortal. Thus when their bodies die, their spirits or souls go either to heaven to live with God or to an eternally burning hell. In other words, people have innate immortality. It is impossible for them to really die or cease to exist.

Many biblical scholars down through history, looking at the issue through Hebrew rather than Greek eyes, have denied the teaching of innate immortality. One such individual was George Storrs. After three years of intensive Bible study, this Methodist minister concluded in 1840 that human beings do not possess inherent immortality. Immortality, he held, belongs to those who follow Christ, and thus it is conditional. Those who accept Christ by faith will have immortality, while those who reject Him remain mortal and subject to death.

That teaching, of course, has direct implications for the fate of the wicked. In short, if the wicked are not immortal, they cannot burn forever. They will be consumed in the fires of hell, and the result will be eternal. Thus Storrs began to preach "annihilationism." To believe anything else, he held, was to impugn the loving character of God.

In 1842 Storrs joined Millerite Adventism and soon developed into one of the movement's leading activists and writers. In the fall of 1844, as we saw earlier, he became one of the foremost advocates of the seventh-month movement. Meanwhile, one of his first ministerial converts was Charles Fitch. "Dear Br. Storrs," Fitch wrote on January 25, 1844, "as you have long been fighting the Lord's battles alone, on the subject of the state of the dead, and of the final doom of the wicked, I write this to say that I am at last after much thought and prayer, and a full conviction of duty to God, prepared to take my stand by your side" (Charles Fitch to George Storrs, Jan. 25, 1844).

The three founders of Seventh-day Adventism—Joseph Bates and James and Ellen White—all accepted the teaching of conditional immortality. To them it not only made biblical sense, but seemed to be necessitated by their theology. After all, a belief in immortal souls already in heaven or hell appeared to do away with the need for the pre- and postmillennial resurrections described in the New Testament. Beyond that, if people already had their reward, why have a pre-Advent judgment or even the Second Advent? Thus conditional immortality formed an integral link in a theology centered on Christ's ministry in the heavenly sanctuary.

The "Pillar" Doctrines and the Three Angels' Messages

By early 1848 the Sabbatarian Adventist leaders, through extensive and intensive Bible study, had come to basic agreement on at least five points of doctrine: (1) the personal, visible, premillennial return of Jesus; (2) the cleansing of the sanctuary, with Christ's ministry in the second apartment having begun on October 22, 1844—the beginning of the antitypical day of atonement; (3) the validity of the gift of prophecy, with progressively more of the believers seeing Ellen White's ministry as a modern manifestation of that gift; (4) the obligation to observe the seventh-day Sabbath and the role of the Sabbath in the great end-time conflict prophesied in Revelation 11-14; and (5) that immortality is not an inherent human quality but something people receive only through faith in Christ.

Sabbatarian Adventists, and later Seventh-day Adventists, came to see those five doctrines as "landmark" or "pillar" tenets. Together they set this branch of Adventism off from not only other Millerite bodies, but from other Christians in general. Those five distinctives stood at the heart of developing Sabbatarian Adventism and made them a distinctive people. As such, the seventh-day people highly valued and avidly preached these beliefs.

The Sabbatarians, of course, shared many beliefs with other Christians, such as salvation by grace through faith in Jesus' sacrifice and the efficacy of prayer. But their preaching and teaching focused on their distinctive pillar doctrines. That emphasis grew partly out of the fact that they had to defend those beliefs in their encounters with other Christians, and partly out of their desire to share those teachings with people who did not know them. As we shall see in chapter 5, that one-sided emphasis eventually led to problems in Adventism.

Meanwhile, it is important to realize that the five pillar doctrines did not stand alone. They formed a unified doctrinal/prophetic package. At the core of that package were two biblical ideas—the sanctuary and the three angels' messages. Of the centrality of the sanctuary in Sabbatarian belief, Roswell F. Cottrell wrote in 1863: "We find, not only that the sanctuary in heaven is the grand center of the Christian system, as the earthly was of the typical, but that this subject is the center and citadel of present truth. And since our temple is in heaven, and in that temple, 'the ark of his testament,' containing 'the commandments of God,' and in the very midst of these commandments, the Sabbath of the Lord, fenced around by nine moral precepts that cannot be overthrown, it is no wonder that the enemies of the Sabbath should, not only strive to abolish the ten commandments, but to demolish the true sanctuary in which they are deposited" (RH, Dec. 15, 1863).

Our previous discussion has pointed out the relationship of each of the landmark doctrines to the sanctuary. At this juncture it is important to emphasize both the centrality of the sanctuary in Adventist theology and the fact that that theology is a unified set of beliefs. Thus to challenge one part of the system questions all of it.

The second organizing and unifying biblical image for Sabbatarian Adventism's theology was that of the three angels of Revelation 14. Those messages not only tied all of Adventist theology to the sanctuary service with its judgment (and salvation) message, but enabled the Sabbatarians to place themselves in the flow of prophetic history. Beyond that, the three angels' messages eventually became the prophetic force that spread Seventh-day Adventist missions throughout the world as the church sought to take its unique message "to every nation, and kindred, and tongue, and people" (Rev. 14:6). But that mission vision was far from the minds of the few struggling Sabbatarian Adventists in the late 1840s.

On the other hand, even then they were beginning to catch the prophetic import of the three angels for their work. In 1850 James White published an important article summarizing their conclusions on the topic. He equated the first angel's message (see verses 6, 7) with the Millerite preaching of the Second Advent. For him the time element in "the *hour* of his judgment is come" was crucial. "The whole Advent host," he penned, "once believed" that something special would happen about 1843. "The unbelief of those who doubt now," he continued, "does not prove that we were all mistaken then. The passing of the time, and the perpetual backsliding and unbelief of Adventists has not changed this truth of God into a lie; but it remains truth still."

The second angel (see verse 8), White emphasized, *"followed"* the first angel. When, in reaction to the preaching of the soon return of Christ, the churches began to shut their doors to the Millerites and disfellowship them, then—under the leadership of Charles Fitch—the second angel sounded with the message of "'Babylon is fallen. . . . Come out of her, my people.'"

"This prophecy," White penned, "was exactly fulfilled, and in the right time, and place. . . . We heard it with our ears, our voices proclaimed it, and our whole being felt its power, and with our eyes we saw its effect, as the oppressed people of God burst the bands that bound them to the various sects, and made their escape from Babylon. . . .

"The second angel's message called us out from the fallen churches where we are now free to think, and act for ourselves in the fear of God. It is an exceedingly interesting fact, that the Sabbath question began to be agitated among second advent believers immediately after they were called out of the churches by the second angel's message. God's work moves in order. The Sabbath truth came up in just the right time to fulfill prophecy."

White saw the message of the third angel (see verses 9-12) as the climax to this prophetic movement. It would be God's last message of mercy to the world just prior to the great harvest of souls at the Second Advent (see verses 15-20).

He pointed out that Revelation 13 and 14 and the message of the third angel recognize only two classes of people. One persecutes the saints and receives the mark of the beast, while the other continues to be patient in waiting for Christ to return (in spite of the October 22, 1844, disappointment) and is "KEEPING THE COMMANDMENTS OF GOD."

"Never did I have such feelings while holding my pen as now," James White wrote as he moved toward his presentation's emotional climax. "And never did I see and feel the importance of the Sabbath as I do this moment. Surely the Sabbath truth, like the rising sun ascending from the east, has increased in light, in power and in importance until it is the great sealing truth. . . .

"Many stopped at the first angel's message, and others at the second, and many will refuse the third; but a few will 'follow the Lamb whithersoever he goeth,' and go up and possess the land. Though they have to pass through fire and blood, or witness the 'time of trouble such as never was,' they will not yield, and 'receive the mark of the beast,' but they will struggle on, and press their holy warfare until they, with the harps of God, strike the note of victory on mount Zion" (PT, April 1850).

Truly the Sabbatarian Adventists saw themselves as a movement of prophecy. Because of their convictions they often referred to their movement as the "third angel's message."

The "Shut Door" Approach to Mission

While the three angels' messages of Revelation 14 obviously pointed to worldwide mission, that aspect of the chapter was not at all evident to the early Sabbatarian Adventists. Truth is progressive, and, as is often the case in our personal lives, the Sabbatarians comprehended God's plan for them only one step at a time. In fact, we might best think of the early Sabbatarian Adventists in terms of antimission rather than mission. We can accurately describe their mission theory and practice as a "shut door" on mission outreach.

That concept was not original with the Sabbatarian believers, but had been developed by William Miller, who had likened his message to the "midnight cry" in the parable of the ten virgins (see Matt. 25). That parable states that when the bridegroom (i.e., Christ) comes, the door will be shut, leaving some on the outside. "'The door was shut,'" Miller taught in the 1830s and early 1840s, "implies the closing up of the mediatorial kingdom, and finishing the gospel period" (*Evidence From Scripture and History* [1842 printing], p. 237). After Christ did not return on October 22, 1844, Miller—still expecting Christ's soon appearance in the clouds of heaven—interpreted the shut door as the close of human probation.

Thus in December 1844 Miller could write: "We have done our work in warning sinners, and in trying to awake a formal church. God, in his providence has shut the door; we can only stir one another up to be *patient;* and be diligent to make our calling and election sure. We are now living in the time specified by Malachi iii.18, also Daniel xii.10, Rev. xxii.10-12. In this passage we cannot help but see, that a little while before Christ should come, there would be a separation between the just and unjust. . . . Never since the days of the apostles, has there been such a division line drawn" (AH, Dec. 11, 1844).

Certainly the nasty reactions of scoffing unbelievers and ex-Millerites after the Great Disappointment must have made it seem that the door of probation had indeed shut. In addition, the massive flow of new converts had come to an abrupt halt on October 22.

Nearly all Millerites accepted the shut-door teaching right after the Great Disappointment. But that soon changed, since the shut-door teaching was tied to the fulfillment of prophecy on October 22. As a result, when the majority of the Millerites, under Himes's leadership, began to claim that they had been wrong on the time and that nothing had happened on October 22, they also gave up their belief that the door of probation had closed.

On the other hand, the Sabbatarian Adventists, including Bates and the Whites, continued to hold to both an October 22 fulfillment of prophecy and the shut-door teaching. Thus the other Millerite Adventists began to refer to them as "the Sabbath and shut-door people"—derogatory terms signifying their doctrinal distinctives.

The problem of the shut-door people was that they had inherited from the Millerite movement some error in their shut-door theory that was intimately tied to their misunderstanding of the cleansing of the sanctuary. After all, if the cleansing of the sanctuary was the second coming of Christ, then probation for the wicked would obviously have closed on October 22. Further Bible study, as we noted above, soon led the Sabbatarians to see their error in regard to the cleansing of the sanctuary, but it took them several years to clear up the related shut-door misconception.

Meanwhile, sometimes even mistakes lead to good results. So it happened with the shut door. During the shut-door period of Adventist mission development Sabbatarian Adventists believed that the evangelistic outreach of their movement was restricted to those who had accepted the Millerite message of the 1830s and early 1840s. The door of mercy had shut for all others.

Thus the shut-door "mistake" provided the small band of Sabbatarian Adventists with ample time to build their own theological foundation. They spent little of their scarce resources on evangelism until they had a message. After sorting out their own theological identity, their next step was to try to convince other Millerites of their doctrinal package and prophetic interpretation. That task took place between 1848 and 1850 (to be covered in the next chapter).

The "utility" of the shut-door period, therefore, was that it allowed time for the Sabbatarians to form a doctrinal foundation and develop a membership base. Only after they had completed those tasks were they ready to take the next step in their prophetic mission.

For Those Who Would Like to Read More

Damsteegt, P. Gerard. *Foundations of the Seventh-day Adventist Message and Mission.* Grand Rapids: Eerdmans, 1977. (Reprinted by Andrews University Press, Berrien Springs, Mich., 1988.)

Douglass, Herbert E. *Messenger of the Lord: The Prophetic Ministry of Ellen G. White.* Boise, Idaho: Pacific Press, 1998.

Froom, LeRoy Edwin. *The Conditionalist Faith of Our Fathers.* Washington, D.C.: Review and Herald, 1965. Vol. 2, pp. 646-740.

Holbrook, Frank B., ed. *Doctrine of the Sanctuary: A Historical Survey (1845-1863).* Silver Spring, Md.: General Conference of Seventh-day Adventists, 1989.

Knight, George R. *Joseph Bates: The Real Founder of Seventh-day Adventism.* Hagerstown, Md.: Review and Herald, 2004.

————. *Meeting Ellen White: A Fresh Look at Her Life, Writings, and Major Themes.* Hagerstown, Md.: Review and Herald, 1996.

————. *A Search for Identity.* Pp. 55-89.

————. *Walking With Ellen White: The Human Interest Story.* Hagerstown, Md.: Review and Herald, 1999.

————, ed. *1844 and the Rise of Sabbatarian Adventism.* Pp. 143-190. (This volume contains most of the documents cited in this chapter.)

Land, Gary, ed. *Adventism in America.* Pp. 29-52.

Maxwell, C. Mervyn. *Tell It to the World.* Pp. 40-94.

Schwarz, Richard W., and Floyd Greenleaf. *Light Bearers.* Pp. 51-68.

Wheeler, Gerald. *James White: Innovator and Overcomer.* Hagerstown, Md.: Review and Herald, 2003.

White, Arthur L. *Ellen G. White.* Washington, D.C.: Review and Herald, 1981-1986. Vol. 1, pp. 45-138.

CHAPTER 3

Era of Organizational Development

(1848-1863)

Looking at the present worldwide Seventh-day Adventist organization, I find it difficult to believe that most of the earliest Adventists opposed all church organization above the congregational level. George Storrs summed up their position nicely when he warned that "no church can be organized by man's invention but what it becomes Babylon *the moment it is organized*" (MC, Feb. 15, 1844).

Storrs' logic is not too difficult to grasp. After all, hadn't the organized churches, the very bodies that Fitch and his followers had defined as Babylon, excommunicated the Millerites? Why, the logic ran, should these free people re-create another Babylon? That sentiment was widespread among all Millerite Adventist branches, including the Sabbatarians. In addition, the strong influence exerted by the Christian Connexion—a group that traditionally had resisted church organization above the local level—also strengthened the antiorganization attitude among Adventists. Two of the three Sabbatarian founders—James White and Joseph Bates—had belonged to the Connexion.

On the other hand, the third founder—Ellen White—had

grown up in the Methodist Episcopal Church. The title of Charles Ferguson's *Organizing to Beat the Devil: Methodists and Early America* helps us see that Mrs. White, coming from the most efficiently organized Protestant denomination of the day, brought a different perspective to the topic. It took nearly 20 years for the tension over organization to find resolution among the Sabbatarian Adventists.

Meanwhile, by 1848, as we saw in chapter 2, the small group of Sabbatarian leaders had agreed on a set of basic doctrines and believed they had a responsibility to share their beliefs with those Adventists still confused about what had taken place in October 1844. The Sabbatarians chose a typically Millerite approach for sharing their beliefs. They organized a series of conferences to discuss the issue. We should regard these semi-informal conferences as the first organizational step in the development of Seventh-day Adventism.

The Sabbatarian Conferences

The first of the Sabbatarian Conferences convened in the spring of 1848 in Rocky Hill, Connecticut. At least five more met that year, another six in 1849, and 10 in 1850. Joseph Bates and the Whites attended most of them. Although most conferences took place over a weekend, some went from Thursday through Monday. Their purpose, according to James White, was the "uniting [of] the brethren on the great truths connected with the message of the third angel" (RH, May 6, 1852). By 1848 many in New England and western New York had become convinced of the validity of one or more of the Sabbatarian Adventist doctrines, but they lacked a common consensus.

James White's report of the first Sabbath conference illustrates both their purpose and some of the dynamics involved. "We had a meeting that evening [Thursday, April 20, 1848] of about fifteen in all," White wrote. "Friday morning the brethren came in until we numbered about fifty. *They were not all fully in the truth.* Our meeting that day was very interesting. *Bro. Bates presented the commandments* in a clear light, and their importance was urged home by powerful testimonies. *The word had effect to establish those already in the truth, and to awaken those who were not fully decided*" (in 2SG 93; italics supplied).

The purpose and dynamics of the conferences came out even more clearly in Ellen White's report of the second one, which met in "Bro. Arnold's barn" in Volney, New York, during August 1848. "There were about thirty-five present," she penned, "all that could be collected in that part of the State. *There were hardly two agreed.* Each was strenuous for his views, declaring that they were according to the Bible. *All were anxious for an opportunity to advance their sentiments, or to preach to us. They were told that we had not come so great a distance to hear them, but had come to teach them the truth.* Bro. Arnold held that the 1000 years of Rev. xx were in the past; and that the 144,000 were those raised at CHRIST's resurrection. . . .

"These strange differences of opinion rolled a heavy weight upon me, especially as Bro. A[rnold] spoke of the 1000 years being in the past. I knew that he was in error, and great grief pressed my spirits; for it seemed to me that GOD was dishonored. I fainted under the burden. Brethren Bates, Chamberlain, Gurney, Edson, and my husband, prayed for me. . . . The LORD heard the prayers of his servants, and I revived. The light of Heaven rested upon me. I was soon lost to earthly things. My accompanying angel presented before me some of the errors of those present, and also the truth in contrast with their errors. That these discordant views, which they claimed to be according to the Bible, were only according to their opinion of the Bible, and that their errors must be yielded, and *they unite upon the third angel's message*. Our meeting ended victoriously. Truth gained the victory" (*ibid.* 97-99; italics supplied).

Note that Bates and the Whites took a strong leadership role early in the conferences. It required forceful, goal-oriented leadership to form a body of believers within the chaotic conditions of post-Disappointment Adventism. Also we should observe that the *primary* purpose of those meetings was to unite a body of believers in the truths of the third angel's message—a message already studied out and agreed upon by the Sabbatarian leaders.

According to James White, by November 1849 the conferences were fulfilling their primary purpose. "By the proclamation of the Sabbath truth in . . . connection with the Advent movement," he reported to a Brother Bowles, "God is making known those that are His. In western N.Y. the number of Sabbath keepers is increasing fast. There are more than twice the number now than six months ago. So it is [also] more or less in Maine, Mass., N.H., Vermont, and Conn. . . .

"*The scattering time* [as a result of the Great Disappointment] *we have had; it is in the past, and now the time for the saints to be gathered into the unity of the faith, and be sealed by one holy, uniting truth has come.* Yes, Brother, it has come.

"It is true that the work moves slowly, but it moves sure, and it gathers strength at every step. . . .

"*Our past Advent experience, and present position and future work is marked out in Rev. 14 Chap. as plain as the prophetic pencil could write it.* Thank God that we see it. . . .

"I believe that the Sabbath truth is yet to ring through the land, as the Advent never has. . . .

"I am sick of all our Advent papers, and all our Advent editors, poor creatures. Lamps gone out, still trying to light their blind brethren to the kingdom of God." James added that he had no desire to be like them. "I only ask the precious privilege to feed, if possible[,] my poor brethren—'the outcasts'" (JW to Brother Bowles, Nov. 8, 1849; italics supplied).

Thus from almost their beginning the Sabbatarians saw

themselves as a mission-driven people, a people propelled by the imperative of the three angels of Revelation 14. The first step in their mission to the world was to reach out to the confused Millerites during the late 1840s. The Sabbatarian conferences became the initial avenue to accomplish that goal.

We should note that while the primary purpose of the Sabbath conferences was to unite the believers in a doctrinal package already studied out, the conferences also provided opportunity to refine those positions as new questions led to further answers in the context of Bible study.

Publishing "the Truth"

The second step in the development of a Sabbatarian organizational structure lay in the area of publications. Like the Sabbatarian Conferences, the initial publications served to call out, inform, and unite a body of believers on the three angels' messages from within the scattered ranks of the still confused Millerite Adventists. Also paralleling the conferences was the fact that publications stood at the heart of predisappointment Millerite "organization."

The first publications of the Sabbatarians were occasional tracts that highlighted their newfound truths in the context of Millerism as a prophetic movement. These tracts, or small books, included Bates's *The Opening Heavens* (1846), *The Seventh-day Sabbath, a Perpetual Sign* (1846 and significantly revised in 1847), *Second Advent Way Marks and High Heaps* (1847), and *A Seal of the Living God* (1849).

Beyond Bates's pamphlets was the first joint publishing venture of the Sabbatarian leadership—*A Word to the "Little Flock"* (1847). The 24-page document encouraged Advent believers to hold on to their 1844 experience as they sought greater light on their future.

An Ellen White vision in Dorchester, Massachusetts, during November 1848 stimulated a major transition in Adventist publishing. After coming out of vision, she told James that she had "a message" for him. "You must begin to print a little paper and send it out to the people. Let it be small at first; but as the people read, they will send you means with which to print, and it will be a success from the first. From this small beginning it was shown to me *to be like streams of light that went clear round the world*" (LS 125; italics supplied).

Her prediction of a worldwide publishing program could not have arisen from anything particularly encouraging among the scattered Sabbatarian believers at that time. Humanly speaking, it looked absurd. What could a few penniless preachers backed by about 100 believers possibly accomplish? Certainly we could not imagine a more humble beginning for a publishing venture.

In spite of the daunting circumstances, the financially prostrate and homeless James White stepped out in faith to write and print the "little paper." Looking back at the experience, he later wrote: "We sat down to prepare the matter for that little sheet, and wrote every word of it, our entire library comprising a three-shilling pocket Bible, Cruden's Condensed Concordance, and Walker's old dictionary, minus one of its covers. Destitute of means, our hope of success was in God" (RH, June 17, 1880).

Not having much choice, White sought out a non-Adventist printer who printed an eight-page pamphlet for a total stranger and waited for his pay until contributions filtered back from the hoped-for readers. White found such a printer in Charles Pelton of Middletown, Connecticut.

The first issue of 1,000 copies of the *Present Truth* came off the press in July 1849. "When he brought the first number from the printing-office," Ellen White recalled, "we all bowed around it, asking the Lord, with humble hearts and many tears, to let his blessing rest upon the feeble efforts of his servant. He [James] then directed the paper to all he thought would read it, and carried it to the post office [eight miles distant] in a carpet-bag. . . . Very soon letters came bringing means to publish the paper, and the good news of many souls embracing the truth" (LS [1888] 260).

The content of the *Present Truth* was what the Sabbatarians saw as the message for that time—the Sabbath, the three angels' messages, and related doctrinal topics. The "little paper" played its part in the "gathering time" of the late 1840s.

The publication of the *Present Truth*, however, was only the first step in the development of Sabbatarian periodicals. The summer of 1850 saw James release the first issue of the *Advent Review*—a journal that reprinted many of the most important Millerite articles of the early 1840s. The *Advent Review* sought to impress the scattered Millerites with the forcefulness and truthfulness of the arguments undergirding the 1844 movement.

November 1850 witnessed the combining of the *Present Truth* and the *Advent Review* into the *Second Advent Review and Sabbath Herald*. That journal, currently known as the *Adventist Review*, truly did become a worldwide periodical that encircles the world today "like streams of light."

For many years the *Review and Herald* (as it was affectionately called) was essentially "the church" for most Sabbatarians. After all, they generally had no church building, denomination, or regular preacher. The periodic arrival of the *Review* provided the scattered Adventists with news of their church and fellow believers, sermons, and a sense of belonging. As such, its influence and importance in early Adventism is almost impossible to overestimate.

The early 1850s saw one other addition to Sabbatarian periodical literature. In 1852 James White began publishing the *Youth's Instructor* (its modern successor is *Insight*) for the youth of the church. The *Youth's Instructor* was the first organized attempt to do something for Sabbatarian young people.

In its train soon followed the establishment of Sabbath schools, for which the *Instructor* published the Bible lessons. The first Sabbath schools began in the 1850s under the leadership of James White, John Byington (who served as the first General Conference president a decade later), and M. G. Kellogg.

By the end of the 1850s the Sabbatarian publishing effort had become a major business venture, establishing its own publishing house in Battle Creek, Michigan, in 1855. The problem of ownership of the publishing enterprise eventually pushed the Sabbatarian Adventists toward a more formal and legal organizational structure.

Early Moves Toward Formal Organization

Because of aggressive outreach through conferences and publications aimed at the large body of searching Millerites, by 1852 the Sabbatarian Adventists were experiencing rapid growth. According to one estimate that seems fairly accurate, their adherents went from about 200 in 1850 to approximately 2,000 in 1852. While that type of growth is a blessing to a religious movement, it brings its own problems.

Thus it should come as no surprise to find the leading Sabbatarians and some local congregations concerning themselves with "gospel order" (church organization) in the early 1850s. They faced several problems. First, they had no way to certify clergy. The scattered congregations were at the mercy of any traveling preacher who claimed to be a Sabbatarian minister. Closely connected to that issue was the fact that Sabbatarians had no channels or provision for ordination. As a result, while James White had been ordained as a minister in the Christian Connexion in 1843, it is probable that Joseph Bates never did receive ordination.

Second, the believers had no way to distribute funds to ministers. In fact, neither did they have any systematic means to gather funds. As we shall soon see, the crisis of an underpaid and demoralized ministry led to the near collapse of the Sabbatarian movement in 1856.

Third, they had no legal organization for holding property. That was not much of a problem in 1850, but by late in the decade it became an issue that they had no choice but to address.

Perhaps the first significant discussions among Sabbatarians regarding gospel order took place in 1850 and 1851. At that time the issue was the withdrawing of the hand of fellowship from members who had become mixed up with spiritualism and other unchristian activities. Then, in the early 1850s, we find congregations ordaining deacons for the celebration of the "ordinances of the Lord's house." That year also witnessed the first formal ordination of men for the gospel ministry. In addition, by 1853 the "leading brethren"—generally Bates and White—were issuing signed identification cards to "traveling brethren" in order to thwart impostors.

The year 1853 also saw James and Ellen White open up their siege guns on the topic of gospel order. "The Lord has shown that gospel order has been too much feared and neglected," Ellen wrote. "Formality should be shunned; but, in so doing, order should not be neglected. There is order in heaven. There was order in the church when Christ was upon the earth. . . . And now in these last days, while God is bringing His children into the unity of the faith, there is more real need of order than ever before" (EW 97).

Underlying her argument seems to be the idea that the church was doing a battle with the highly organized forces of evil. Therefore, the only way to win the conflict was for the church to organize so as not to be outmaneuvered. For that reason Satan was busy seeking to prevent and destroy rational gospel order among the Sabbatarians.

December 1853 also found James White firing off a salvo of four articles on church organization in the *Review*. In the first he hit hard at the antiorganization members in the Sabbatarian group. By seeking to avoid becoming "Babylon" through organization, he charged, they were themselves in a state of "perfect Babylon" or confusion (RH, Dec. 6, 1853).

While the Whites had launched their battle for gospel order in 1853, it took another decade to achieve their goal.

"Sister Betsy" and Support for the Ministry

By the fall of 1856 a crisis of the first magnitude had developed in Adventism. The Lord had not come, and some were experiencing spiritual decline. It was especially evident among several of the most promising young Sabbatarian preachers. The men were both overworked and underpaid—a sure combination to break a person's spirit.

A case in point was young John Nevins Andrews, a man who later served the church as its leading scholar, its first "official" foreign missionary, and its General Conference president. But in the mid-1850s overwork and deprivation had forced him into an early retirement (he was in his mid-20s). As Andrews put it: "'In less than five years [after beginning his public ministry] I was utterly prostrated'" (CTemp 263). The fall of 1856 found Andrews deciding to leave the ministry to become a clerk in his uncle's store in Waukon, Iowa. Waukon, we should note, was rapidly becoming a colony of apathetic Sabbatarian Adventists.

Another leading minister to retire to Waukon in 1856 was John Loughborough. He had become, as he put it, "somewhat discouraged as to finances" (*Rise and Progress of SDAs*, p. 208).

The Whites temporarily averted a crisis in the Adventist

ministry by making a danger-filled midwinter journey to Waukon to wake up the sleeping Adventist community and to reclaim the dropout ministers. Both Andrews and Loughborough saw the hand of God in the visit and rededicated their lives to preaching the third angel's message.

Their rededication, of course, did not change the objective financial facts. For example, for his first three months' labor after leaving Waukon, Loughborough received room and board, a buffalo-skin overcoat worth about $10, and $10 in cash as pay for his ministerial labor. The problem was far from solved.

Anticipating the financial problems, the Battle Creek congregation (the most influential Sabbatarian congregation) formed a study group in the spring of 1858 to search the Scriptures for a plan to support the ministry. Under the leadership of J. N. Andrews, the group made a report in early 1859. They proposed a plan that came to be known as Systematic Benevolence (or "Sister Betsy," as many soon nicknamed it).

The plan encouraged men to contribute five to 25 cents per week, and women two to 10 cents. In addition, both groups were assessed one to five cents per week for each $100 worth of property.

James White was jubilant over the plan, estimating that the 1,000 potential givers in Michigan alone could contribute $5,980 a year, enough to send five "missionaries" to the West, "to sustain the cause in this State," and yet without "any privation [to the giver] of the necessaries of life" (RH, May 26, 1859).

While "Sister Betsy" did not match up to the tithing plan that Seventh-day Adventists eventually adopted after further Bible study in the late 1870s, it was a first step in the systematic support of the church and a further development in the movement toward formal organization by the Sabbatarians.

The Final Drive for Church Organization

By the summer of 1859 James White was ready to open the final drive for formal denominational organization. In a July 21 *Review* editorial he penned, "We lack system. And we should not be afraid of that system which is not opposed by the Bible, and is approved by sound sense. The lack of system is felt everywhere." He then went on to make some suggestions that would bring order out of chaos.

"We are aware that these suggestions," White continued, "will not meet the minds of all. Bro. Over-cautious will be frightened, and will be ready to warn his brethren to be careful and not venture out too far; while Bro. Confusion will cry out, 'O, this looks just like Babylon! Following the fallen church!' Bro. Do-little will say, 'The cause is the Lord's, and we had better leave it in his hands, he will take care of it.' 'Amen,' says Love-this-world, Slothful, Selfish, and Stingy, 'if God calls men to preach, let them go out and preach, he will take care of them, and those who believe their message;' while Korah, Dathan and Abiram are ready to rebel against those who feel the weight of the cause, and who watch for souls as those who must give account, and raise the cry, 'Ye take too much upon you'" (RH, July 21, 1859).

The time for soft-spoken speeches had obviously passed, but the battle for organization was far from over. That became evident to all readers of the *Review* in early 1860. In February James White raised the questions of forming a legal organization to hold property and of adopting a name for the developing denomination. The two issues were intimately related, since it was necessary to provide a name for the organization if it was to be legally incorporated in the state of Michigan and legally empowered to own the Adventist publishing house and the Battle Creek church building.

White's suggestion brought forth a broadside from R. F.

Cottrell—a corresponding editor of the *Review* and the leader of those opposed to church organization. Cottrell wrote that he believed "it would be wrong to 'make us a name,' since that lies at the foundation of Babylon. I do not think that God would approve of it" (RH, Mar. 22, 1860).

Published during White's absence from the editorial office, the article by an experienced and influential Sabbatarian Adventist leader set the stage for a long, drawn-out battle. For the next six months nearly every issue of the *Review* had some material on the problem as the church hammered out a solution in the public forum.

The leading ministers called a "general conference" of the Sabbatarians for September 28 to October 1, 1860. At that meeting, despite the impassioned airing of the "Babylon" arguments, those present decided to incorporate the publishing house. Beyond that, they adopted the name "Seventh-day Adventist" as best representing the beliefs of the evolving denomination. The next step was the incorporation of the Seventh-day Adventist Publishing Association on May 3, 1861, under the laws of the state of Michigan.

Thus a major battle had been won on the organizational front. At that point complete victory was not far off, even though in August 1861 James White complained of "a stupid uncertainty upon the subject of organization" (RH, Aug. 27, 1861).

In October the Michigan Conference of Seventh-day Adventists formed, with William A. Higley (a layman) as president. With the logjam finally broken, 1862 saw the organization of seven more local conferences: Southern Iowa (March 16), Northern Iowa (May 10), Vermont (June 15), Illinois (September 28), Wisconsin (September 28), Minnesota (October 4), and New York (October 25). Others soon followed.

The final step in the development of church organization took place in a meeting of representatives of the local conferences at Battle Creek in May 1863. At that time the General Conference of Seventh-day Adventists came into being, with John Byington as its first president. James White had been the unanimous choice for the denomination's presidency, but he wisely declined the office because of his forceful role in urging organization.

In 1863 the newly formed Seventh-day Adventist Church had about 3,500 members and about 30 ministers. Thus it was possible for the president of the General Conference to direct the detailed work of the church personally. This changed during the next four decades as membership increased, as the church developed major institutions, and as it went worldwide in its mission.

We will return to the development of church organization in chapter 6. Meanwhile, we need to examine how this shut-door antimission group eventually became a worldwide missionary movement.

The "Shut Door" Cracks Open a Little

We will recall from chapter 2 that the Sabbatarian Adventists, following Miller's lead, believed that the door of mercy had closed in October 1844 for all but those who had accepted the soon coming of Jesus before the Great Disappointment. Thus the Sabbatarians' only mission outreach for the next few years involved Millerites and ex-Millerites. Their concept of mission was extremely narrow.

Apparently all the leading Sabbatarians shared that "antimission" mentality. In 1874, for example, Ellen White wrote: "With my brethren and sisters, after the time passed in forty-four I did believe no more sinners would be converted. But," she was quick to add, "I never had a vision that no more sinners would be converted" (1SM 74). To the contrary, some of her earliest visions indicated further evangelism of a worldwide nature. That was especially true of her 1848 publishing vision

A Brief Look at Adventist History

All photos courtesy of Review and Herald files unless otherwise credited.

William Miller

Joshua V. Himes

Ellen G. White

James White

Joseph Bates

Uriah Smith, longtime editor of the *Review and Herald*, now the *Adventist Review*

John Nevins Andrews, first foreign missionary and leading scholar

The Adventist publishing house in Switzerland

Delegates at the Minneapolis
General Conference session of 1888

E. J. Waggoner

A. T. Jones

John Harvey
Kellogg

The famous Battle Creek Sanitarium at the beginning of the twentieth century

A baptism of 393 persons by 13 pastors in the Phillippines illustrating the explosive growth of the twentieth century

A pioneer woman pastor and evangelist, Minnie Sype

L. Flora Plummer, a pioneer in the Sabbath school program and a long-time director of the General Conference Sabbath School Department

Charles E. Bradford,
first Black president of the
North American Division

Radio Evangelist
H.M.S. Richards

Pioneer Black leader
Frank L. Peterson

Photo by Joel D. Springer

Sabbath services in the Hoosier Dome at the 1990 General Conference session in Indianapolis, Indiana

Photo by Joel D. Springer

General Conference of Seventh-day Adventists headquarters in Silver Spring, Maryland

in which she saw the future of Adventist publications "like streams of light that went clear round the world" (LS 125). However, neither she nor the other Sabbatarians understood its full implications at the time.

By early 1849 Ellen White had begun to tie shut-door terminology to the heavenly sanctuary as the Sabbatarians progressively came to understand both their message and their mission to the world. "I saw," she wrote, "that Jesus had shut the door of the holy place, and no man can open it; and that He had opened the door into the most holy, and no man can shut it" (EW 42). She always believed that those who had rejected the Holy Spirit after being convicted of the truth of the 1844 movement had put themselves beyond God's mercy, but she, along with other Sabbatarians, *gradually* corrected her view of the shut door during the early 1850s.

Part of the reason for the change on the shut door came from the unexpected fact of new conversions to Sabbatarian Adventism. For example, in 1850 James White reported, undoubtedly in surprise, the accession of a man who "had made no public profession of religion" before 1845 (AR, August 1850). Such conversions increased during the next two years. That fact led to a course correction in Adventist theology. By February 1852 James had switched to an open-door evangelistic policy. "This OPEN DOOR we teach, and invite those who have an ear to hear to come to it and find salvation through Jesus Christ. There is an exceeding glory in the view that Jesus has OPENED THE DOOR into the holiest of all. . . . If it be said that we are of the OPEN DOOR and seventh day Sabbath theory, we shall not object; for this is our faith" (RH, Feb. 17, 1852).

Thus the shut-door people became the open-door people as they slowly recognized that the opening of the final phase of Christ's ministry in the Most Holy Place of the heavenly sanctuary included the opening of a new message on the Sabbath and the third angel's message. Those realizations eventually propelled the denomination around the world and made missions one of the foremost marks of Seventh-day Adventism. However, such a vision took time to develop.

In the meantime, it is important to note the utility of the shut-door error. Sabbatarian Adventists had inherited it from William Miller along with his mistaken ideas on the sanctuary and its cleansing (the ideas were all tied together). *Gradually*, as they cleared up the errors, the picture came into focus. But we must understand that change as a process rather than as an instantaneous point in time.

By the early 1850s the major pieces were in place. The error on mission was helpful in that it provided the Sabbatarians with time to build both a doctrinal and a population base for the next step in their mission program. By the late 1850s the evolving denomination had also developed a publication, financial, and organizational base from which to launch its mission. But its members were still not ready to act.

Even though the Sabbatarians in the early 1850s held that their unique function in prophetic history was to preach the three angels' messages of Revelation 14, and even though Revelation 14:6 plainly stated that the mission of the first angel was to go "to every nation, and kindred, and tongue, and people," they still held back from worldwide evangelism.

In part, that undoubtedly resulted from their small membership and limited financial resources, but there were other reasons. For one thing, some of the Sabbatarians believed that the Millerites had accomplished the preaching of the first angel's message to all the earth through the sending of their publications around the world.

Other Sabbatarians followed the lead of Uriah Smith, editor of the *Review*. In 1859 someone asked Smith if "the Third Angel's Message [was] being given, or to be given except in the

United States?" Smith replied that even though analogy might lead to the conclusion that the proclamation of the third angel's message might be coextensive with the preaching of the first angel (that is, worldwide), "this might not perhaps be necessary to fulfill Rev. x.11, since our own land is composed of people from almost every nation" (RH, Feb. 3, 1859). Smith's rationale, borrowed from William Miller, was that the gospel merely needed to be preached to a *representative* from each nation. Since the United States was a conglomeration of representative individuals from many nations, foreign missions might not be required.

Thus, although the shut door had begun to open, it had not opened very far. The Sabbatarian Adventists were reluctant missionaries at best. But that was to change dramatically by the end of the century.

For Those Who Would Like to Read More

Knight, George R. *Organizing for Mission and Growth: The Development of Adventist Church Structure*. Hagerstown, Md.: Review and Herald, 2006. Pp. 15-63.

Maxwell, C. Mervyn, *Tell It to the World*. Pp. 95-105, 125-146.

Mustard, Andrew G. *James White and SDA Organization: Historical Development, 1844-1881*. Berrien Springs, Mich.: Andrews University Press, 1988.

Neufeld, Don F., ed. *Seventh-day Adventist Encyclopedia*. 1996 ed. Vol. 11, pp. 249-252, 258-270.

Schwarz, Richard W., and Floyd Greenleaf. *Light Bearers*. Pp. 69-99.

Strayer, Brian E. *J. N. Loughborough: Last of the Adventist Pioneers*. Hagerstown, Md.: Review and Herald, 2013.

White, Arthur L. *Ellen G. White*. Vol. 1, pp. 139-151, 163-178, 256-270, 380-393, 420-431, 445-461; vol. 2, pp. 23-33.

CHAPTER 4

Era of Institutional and Lifestyle Development

(1863-1888)

So far in our study we have seen that the development of Adventism was progressive, with each stage building upon the previous ones. Thus the Millerite movement laid the prophetic base during the period up through October 1844. Between 1844 and 1848 the founders of Seventh-day Adventism erected their distinctive doctrinal framework on the prophetic platform established by Miller. When they had completed that task, the Sabbatarians were ready to organize in order to preserve their beliefs and heritage better and to facilitate their outreach to others. Running parallel to these basic stages was an evolving concept of mission.

The year 1863 witnessed a major shift as Adventists began to focus on the type of life they should live and to develop institutions to support that lifestyle. The years between 1863 and 1888 also brought major changes in Adventist thinking concerning mission to the world.

Healthful Living and the Western Health Reform Institute

The struggle for church organization came to fruition on

May 21, 1863, with the establishment of the General Conference of Seventh-day Adventists. Now the time had arrived for the next step in the formation of Adventism. The first major move in that direction was in the area of healthful living.

A mere 15 days after the achievement of a functional organization, on June 5, 1863, Ellen White received her first comprehensive health reform vision. That vision eventually provided the material for extensive publications on healthful living, but in a letter written the next day she spelled out the vision's essential principles.

"*I saw,*" she wrote, "*that it was a sacred duty to attend to our health, and arouse others to their duty*. . . . We have a duty to speak, to come out against intemperance of every kind—intemperance in working, in eating, in drinking, and in drugging—and then point them to God's great medicine: water, pure soft water, for diseases, for health, for cleanliness, and for luxury. . . . I saw that we should not be silent upon the subject of health but should wake up minds to the subject." "The work God requires of us," she noted, "will not shut us away from caring for our health. *The more perfect our health, the more perfect will be our labor*" (MS 1 1863; italics supplied).

The 1863 vision, however, was not the first stirring of health reform among the early Sabbatarian Adventists. The much-esteemed Joseph Bates, for example, had been an all-around health reformer for many years. During the early 1820s, while still a sea captain, he had given up strong drink when he realized that he looked forward to his daily glass with more enthusiasm than he did to his food. A year later he abandoned wine. Then, after his baptism in 1827, he helped organize one of the first temperance societies in the United States. Subsequent years saw the captain discard tea, coffee, meat, and highly seasoned foods. In their place he sought a plain, wholesome diet. Thus, by the time Bates became a Sabbatarian Adventist, he had already been a health reformer for many years.

Bates, however, did not regard health reform of equal importance to such issues as the seventh-day Sabbath, Christ's heavenly ministry, or the three angels' messages. It was important, but not "present truth." He therefore remained largely silent on the topic until 1863. James White noted that when anyone asked Bates why he did not use certain items, he would reply: "'I have eaten my share of them.'" But he did not make health reform an issue "in public at that time, nor in private, unless questioned upon the subject" (CTemp 252).

Some slight stirrings appeared among other Sabbatarian Adventists on the topic of healthful living in the late 1840s and during the 1850s. In 1848, for example, Mrs. White spoke of the harmful effects of tobacco, tea, and coffee. And in the 1850s the church took some action against tobacco usage. But health reform was marginal and minimal as the evolving denomination wrestled with weightier matters.

One of the most interesting examples of the dynamic, developing quality of "present truth" among the early Adventists is the topic of unclean foods. In November 1850 James White argued extensively, on the basis of Acts 10 and other texts, that pork was a permissible food in the gospel dispensation. He reprinted the article in the *Review* in 1854, apparently because some zealous Adventists kept raising the issue. Finally, in 1858, Ellen White rebuked S. N. Haskell for agitating the question. Her argument is quite interesting. First, she noted that if he kept his ideas on swine's flesh to himself, they would do no harm. But because he was not quiet on the topic, he was causing disruption in the church.

"If it is the duty of the church to abstain from swine's flesh," she continued, "God will discover it to more than two or three. He will teach His *church* their duty.

"God is leading out a people, not a few separate individuals here and there, one believing this thing, another that. . . . The third angel is leading out and purifying a people, and they should move with him unitedly. . . . I saw that the angels of God would lead His people no faster than they could receive and act upon the important truths that are communicated to them" (1T 206, 207).

That is a remarkable statement in that it highlights the facts that (1) God works with groups (churches) and not just individuals, (2) God is patient in His leadership, and (3) present truth is dynamic and progressive—topics that are divisive in one period of a church's history may become important once it has cared for other issues.

Thus it was with health reform. Once the doctrinal and organizational steps were in place, lifestyle issues (including health reform) became the next step in the development of Adventism and present truth. Truth is progressive. God leads His people step by step. Thus a major turning point in Adventist history took place in 1863.

At this juncture we should note that Seventh-day Adventists were not alone in most of their health reform ideas and practices. To the contrary, they were part of a large contemporary health reform movement in the United States. It sought to correct destructive living habits and gross ignorance on how to live and care for one's body. Many of its points we today regard as common knowledge—ideas such as frequent bathing, germs as a cause of disease, the harmful effects of tobacco, the danger of certain types of drugs, and the importance of a balanced diet. But great ignorance reigned on these subjects in mid-nineteenth-century America, and many zealous health reformers arose to combat such misunderstandings. Thus Adventists did not stand alone.

Sylvester Graham, for example, already taught much of the "Adventist" health reform package in the late 1830s. And such reform institutions as Dr. James C. Jackson's Our Home on the Hillside in Dansville, New York, pioneered in providing reform health care and instruction to those who temporarily lived at the institution as patients. Such places were forerunners of the Adventist sanitariums.

Ellen White's June 5, 1863, vision placed Adventists in the health reform movement. Unfortunately, it was easier to read about health reform than it was to live it. As a result, an overworked and intemperate General Conference president by the name of James White suffered a paralytic stroke on August 16, 1865. His wife decided to take James for treatment to Dr. Jackson's institution in Dansville. Two other ailing Adventist leaders—J. N. Loughborough and Uriah Smith—accompanied them. Meanwhile, the 73-year-old health-reforming Bates continued to carry on in good health.

If Adventism came near to collapsing in 1856 because of a lack of organization and an inability to pay its ministers, in 1865 it teetered on the brink of disaster from the poor health habits of its leading ministers. Health reform was not just a strange aberration; it was a crucial necessity.

The next step in Adventism's developing relationship with health reform resulted from Ellen White's vision of December 25, 1865. Her vision called for Adventists to establish their own health reform institution. Beyond that, it integrated health reform into Adventist theology. "The health reform," Mrs. White observed, "is a part of the third angel's message and is just as closely connected with it as are the arm and hand with the human body" (1T 486). Part of the function of health reform, she said, was to prepare people for translation at the second coming of Jesus. Thus, as J. H. Waggoner noted in 1866, health reform was "an essential part of *present truth*" (RH, Aug. 7, 1866).

From 1865 onward, health reform and health care became

growing aspects of Adventist ministry to the church and the world. The *Health Reformer*, a 16-page monthly journal, began in 1866, and the same year saw the establishment of the Western Health Reform Institute in Battle Creek, Michigan. It was the first of what eventually became hundreds of Seventh-day Adventist health-care institutions.

The year 1876 witnessed the appointment of 24-year-old John Harvey Kellogg as chief administrator of the Western Health Reform Institute. Within a few months Kellogg had changed the institution's name to the Battle Creek Sanitarium. The word *sanitarium*, he proclaimed, meant a "place where people learn to stay well." By the 1890s, under Kellogg's guidance, the Battle Creek Sanitarium became the largest institution of its kind in the world and achieved worldwide renown.

The Struggle for Noncombatancy

A second lifestyle issue confronting the newly organized denomination concerned military service. America's bloodiest war began in 1861 and raged on for four years. Two questions presented themselves: Should Adventist men serve in the military? If the answer to that question was yes, then should they bear arms and kill other human beings?

James White opened up the explosive issue in the August 12, 1862, *Review*. The problem, as he saw it, was that "the requirements of war" were out of harmony with "the ten commandments. . . . The fourth precept of the law says, 'Remember the Sabbath day to keep it holy'; the sixth says, 'Thou shalt not kill.'"

After carefully laying out the case, White made an extremely controversial suggestion. "In the case of drafting," he said, "the government assumes the responsibility of the violation of the law of God, and it would be madness to resist. He who would resist until, in the administration of military law, he was shot down, goes too far, we think, in taking the responsibility of suicide" (RH, Aug. 12, 1862).

White's editorial set off a barrage of correspondence. Two weeks later he reported that some members had reacted "in rather a feverish style," essentially charging him with Sabbathbreaking and murder. He added that if any of the Adventist draft resisters chose "to have a clinch with Uncle Sam rather than to obey," they could try it. James claimed that he had no burden to contend with them, "lest some of you non-resistants get up a little war before you are called upon to fight for your country." He added that "any well-written articles, calculated to shed light upon our duty as a people in reference to the present war, will receive prompt attention" (RH, Aug. 26, 1862).

His invitation brought a flood of submissions. The next four months witnessed the debate carried out publicly through the pages of the incipient denomination's major periodical. The discussion covered nearly every possible option. Some respondents saw Daniel in the lions' den and the three Hebrews in the fiery furnace as the correct biblical parallel to the draft. At the opposite extreme were those who, following White's initial lead, claimed that the true biblical parallel lay in the helplessness of the Hebrew slaves in Egypt. According to their argument, such servitude made it impossible to hold the slaves responsible for Sabbathbreaking.

The most radical of the views was that of Joseph Clarke, who wanted to see the "treason" of the South "receive its just deserts." Dreaming of "Gideons, and Jepthas, and fighting Davids," Clarke put the war in covenant perspective by fancying "a regiment of Sabbath-keepers [who] would strike this rebellion a staggering blow, in the strength of Him who always helped His valiant people when they kept His statutes" (RH, Sept. 23, 1862). On the other hand, Henry E. Carver took the pacifist position "that under no circumstances was it justifiable in a follower of the Lamb to use carnal weapons to take the lives of his fellow-men" (RH, Oct. 21, 1862).

By the end of the war the Seventh-day Adventist Church and the United States government had reached a satisfactory solution for members of the young denomination. For its part, the government developed provisions for drafted conscientious believers to do hospital and other work that provided opportunity for them to serve the nation without killing. In exchange, the church advised its members to help their country in times of crisis. Thus by 1864 the government had opened noncombatant options. The denomination had organized just in time to receive official recognition and thus make the noncombatant option available to its members.

Adventism assumed its historic position on military service in 1864. While encouraging its young people not to volunteer, the church since the 1860s has supported noncombatant conscientious cooperation with the military service for its drafted members. On the other hand, reflecting the tension of the early debates, the church has continued to recognize that the responsibility to choose among various military options rests with each individual conscience.

In Search of Proper Education

A third lifestyle/institutional development between 1863 and 1888 centered on Christian education. The educational emphasis came later than other developments, because religious groups focusing on the nearness of the end of the world have generally not felt much need for educating their children. After all, the logic runs, "why send children to school if the world is soon to end and they will never grow up to use their hard-earned learning?"

That attitude was widespread among Adventists. As late as 1862 a church member wrote James White asking Is it "right and consistent for us who believe with all our hearts in the immediate coming of the Lord, to seek to give our children an education? If so, should we send them to a district or town school, where they learn twice as much evil as good?"

White replied that "the fact that Christ is very soon coming is no reason why the mind should not be improved. A *well-disciplined and informed mind can best receive and cherish the sublime truths of the Second Advent*" (RH, Dec. 23, 1862; italics supplied). His reply indicates a part of the rationale that later became the foundation for developing an Adventist system of schools. In addition, the question demonstrates an early distrust of public schools.

By the mid-1850s the problem of schooling had begun troubling some Adventists to the extent that they decided to try their hand at independent Christian schools. The first such endeavor took place at Buck's Bridge, New York, in 1853; the second was in Battle Creek, Michigan, in 1856. But both one-room schools failed after operating for about three years each.

In 1861, when James White faced pressure to establish another school in Battle Creek, he wrote: "We have had a thorough trial of a school at Battle Creek, under most favorable circumstances, and have given it up, as it failed to meet the expectations of those interested" (RH, Sept. 24, 1861). Apparently no further attempts at Adventist schooling occurred until the late 1860s. Meanwhile, the church provided for the religious education of its young people through the pages of the *Youth's Instructor* and through the Sabbath school with its weekly lessons.

By 1867 the Battle Creek Adventists were again ready to establish a school, this time under the leadership of Goodloe Harper Bell, an experienced public school teacher. The school existed sporadically until 1870 or 1871.

In 1872 the denomination began to consider more seriously the need for a quality school—not so much for elementary children as for older students who required an education in order to spread the Adventist message. The church's leadership decided to inaugurate a school at Battle Creek under the financial sponsorship of the General Conference. It would "thoroughly" acquaint its students "with the teachings of the Bible in reference to those great truths which pertain to this time," and provide enough general knowledge to enable them to spread the Adventist message (RH, May 7, 1872).

The Battle Creek school, the first one to have denominational support, opened in June 1872 with Bell teaching 12 students. In 1874 that small beginning became Battle Creek College, with Sidney Brownsberger as principal. Battle Creek College was an important institution in Adventist education history, not only because of its pioneering status, but because it received a great deal of attention in terms of what an Adventist school should accomplish.

General Conference president George I. Butler and the school committee stressed that the purpose of the school was to teach the Bible. The emphasis was to be on both the Adventist doctrinal/prophetic perspectives and those skills necessary to do evangelism of all kinds. They wanted a school centered on the Word of God, Butler said, not a school that focused on traditional learning like others in the land. "We want hundreds of our people to take three, six, twelve, eighteen, or twenty-four months' schooling, as soon as they can consistently do so" (RH, July 21, 1874).

Ellen White penned an important article entitled "Proper Education" to help guide the planning of the new school. Assuming that the school would highlight the Bible, she emphasized that it should aim at developing in its students a balance of mental, physical, and spiritual powers. She particularly stressed the need for a practical education that connected physical labor with academic work.

Many other nineteenth-century reformers also supported such concepts. The major problem with implementing the reform ideals in the Adventist Church was that Adventism lacked educators familiar with them. As a result, Battle Creek College became a traditional rather than a reform-oriented institution. Students in the college's most important course of studies had to spend four to six years on the Latin and Greek classics (the "heathen authors") in order to earn the B.A. degree. The school had no manual labor curriculum, no required Bible class, and no reform program. Battle Creek College's historian has claimed that the school's curriculum was a "philosophic betrayal" (E. K. VandeVere, *The Wisdom Seekers*, p. 23).

Unfortunately, the situation got even worse during the early 1880s. By the summer of 1882 the college's governing board decided to close the school indefinitely. Thus the denomination's first official attempt at formal education collapsed.

Battle Creek College reopened in the autumn of 1883 with a renewed determination to implement Christian principles of education. In spite of significant improvement, however, at no time during the 1880s did the college displace the centrality of the "heathen" classics or fully implement a reform curriculum.

Fortunately, the hard lessons learned at Battle Creek College in the 1870s were not lost on the denomination's budding educational understanding. The spring of 1882 witnessed the establishment of two church-sponsored secondary schools—Healdsburg Academy in California and South Lancaster Academy in Massachusetts. Healdsburg Academy became Healdsburg College the following year and is known today as Pacific Union College. South Lancaster Academy eventually grew into Atlantic Union College.

Brownsberger and Bell, the leading educators at Battle

Creek College during the 1870s, each established one of the schools. Having learned from their previous experience, they made large strides toward implementing the reform curriculum. Thoroughgoing reform, however, awaited the 1890s. The development of an elementary system also did not begin until then.

Advances in Financial Stewardship

It did not take too long for the denomination to discover the weaknesses of Systematic Benevolence. "Sister Betsy" was inadequate and cumbersome, and lacked a firm biblical base.

Gradually during the 1860s and 1870s the denomination evolved a better grasp of true tithing. The issue came to maturity in early 1876, when Dudley M. Canright published a series of *Review* articles emphasizing that Malachi 3:8-11 set forth "the Bible plan of supporting the Ministry." "God requires," he argued, "that a tithe, or one-tenth, of all the income of his people shall be given to support his servants in their labors" (RH, Feb. 17, 1876).

Canright shared his arguments at the General Conference session that November, estimating that if all Adventists paid a faithful tithe, the General Conference treasury would receive $150,000 annually instead of $40,000. As a result of his presentations, the session resolved that it was the duty of all members "under ordinary circumstances, to devote one-tenth of all their income from whatever source, to the cause of God" (RH, Apr. 6, 1876). From that point forward, Seventh-day Adventists increasingly practiced biblical tithing.

Ellen White's Role in the Development of Adventist Lifestyle

We pointed out in chapter 2 that Ellen White did not take a leading role in the development of Adventist doctrine during the 1840s. Rather, the procedure was one of Bible study until a general consensus developed. At that point Ellen White sometimes received a vision that reaffirmed the consensus and helped those who still had questions to accept the correctness of the biblically derived conclusions of the group. Thus we can best think of Mrs. White's involvement in the formation of doctrine as one of confirmation rather than initiation.

The same picture does not hold true for Ellen White's part in the area of Adventist lifestyle. Even though twenty-first-century Adventists have tended to see doctrinal and lifestyle issues as being of equal magnitude, that was not the position of the denomination's founders. Whereas they hammered out the basic doctrines through intensive Bible study and held conferences to bring about consensus, lifestyle development followed a somewhat different pattern. The formation of lifestyle positions was much more casual.

Perhaps the difference revolved around the fact that doctrines define a denomination. Doctrine among early Sabbatarian Adventists, therefore, was a crucial issue and received a great deal of attention. Lifestyle items, on the other hand, tend to be second-order concerns for a denomination. Many lifestyle issues are not so much basic determiners of a denomination's identity as they are ways of life that facilitate its mission in spreading its doctrinal message.

From this perspective, health reform enables people to become better missionaries and enables healthy and healed people to come to the place where they can better understand the gospel. Similarly, Christian education facilitates the development of both individual church members and gospel preachers. On the other hand, when viewed from the perspective of salvation and a relationship with God, doctrines are generally closer to being ends in themselves than are lifestyle issues. Lifestyle issues should be regarded as means to the end of preaching doctrine in the context of salvation.

While the minds of the founders of Adventism may not have consciously followed such reasoning, the movement's early leaders seem to have acted upon it. Thus they made a great deal of effort to state their doctrines precisely, while basically neglecting most lifestyle issues until necessity and crisis forced them to take a position.

Adventists filled the resulting lifestyle void in various ways, depending on the issue. Sometimes a position developed through Bible study and conferences as a crisis arose, but at other times Ellen White took the lead in raising the issue, pointing to the solution, and indicating how that solution fit into the larger picture of the three angels' messages.

That latter course was evident in the area of health reform, while the former predominated in such areas as military service and tithing. Because Ellen White often applied biblical principles to the everyday life of the church and its individual believers, over the years her counsel has come increasingly to the center of any discussion of Adventist lifestyle.

In summary, we find in the development of early Adventism a dual role for Ellen White, with less activity in the realm of doctrinal formation and more in lifestyle development.

Missions: Foreign and Not So Foreign

We noted in chapters 2 and 3 that early Seventh-day Adventists were anything but enthusiastic missionaries. And that in spite of the fact that the focal point of their preaching was the three messages of Revelation 14 with its obvious imperative for worldwide mission. Early Adventists gave up the shut door only because the presence of new converts forced them to do so. Even after that, they continued to minimize their mission responsibility.

As on so many occasions, James White stood at the forefront of those who envisioned a larger work for the denomination. A month before the organization of the General Conference in 1863, White claimed in the *Review* that "ours is a world-wide message" (RH, Apr. 21, 1863). A few months earlier he had pointed out the need for sending a missionary to Europe. Then, in June 1863, the *Review* reported that "the General Conference Executive Committee may send him [B. F. Snook] a missionary to Europe before the close of 1863" (RH, June 2, 1863).

While the newly established General Conference did not have enough staff to permit them to dispatch Snook overseas, it did have a minister who was more than eager for the assignment. In 1858 Michael Belina Czechowski (an ex-Roman Catholic Polish priest who had converted to Adventism in America in 1857) wrote, "How I would love to visit my own native country across the big waters, and tell them about Jesus' coming, and the glorious restitution, and how they must keep the Commandments of God and the Faith of Jesus" (RH, Sept. 23, 1858). Because of the newness of his faith, perceived personal instabilities, and other reasons, the church refused to send Czechowski as a missionary.

In frustration the creative Pole requested and received missionary sponsorship from the Advent Christian denomination (the main body of Sundaykeeping Adventists). After arriving in Europe in 1864, Czechowski preached the Seventh-day Adventist message in spite of his Advent Christian sponsorship. He promoted his work through public evangelism, publishing a periodical, and the preparation and circulation of tracts. The effective but erratic preacher planted Seventh-day Adventist doctrinal seeds in Switzerland, Italy, Hungary, Romania, and other parts of Europe, seeds that eventually bore fruit.

Meanwhile, Seventh-day Adventists, still reluctant missionaries at best, took the "adventurous" step in 1868 of sending John N. Loughborough and D. T. Bordeau to far-off

California. The primary impetus for that appointment was a plea from the few Adventist emigrants in that state for a minister. Within a short time of their arrival in San Francisco, a man from a neighboring town met them and claimed that a friend had had an impressive dream in which he saw the two tent evangelists and was told to help them.

From that providential beginning the work grew rapidly in California and the surrounding states. It is of some interest to note that California set the pattern for Adventist missions around the world. After establishing a small population base, the Adventists established a publishing house (the Pacific Press) and a periodical *(Signs of the Times)* in 1874, a sanitarium at St. Helena in 1878, and an academy/college in Healdsburg in 1882. That institutional base actually patterned itself after the Battle Creek experience, and it remains at the heart of Adventist mission strategy to the present day.

Meanwhile, the year after the initiation of the California mission, Czechowski's converts made a move that forced the hesitant Adventist Church to expand its missiological understandings and practices. Czechowski's followers in Switzerland accidentally discovered the existence of the Seventh-day Adventist Church in the United States. Although it upset Czechowski himself, the correspondence eventually led the American Adventist leadership to invite a Swiss representative to the 1869 General Conference session.

He arrived too late for the session, but he remained in the United States for more than a year to become better grounded in Adventist beliefs. Then he returned to Europe in 1870 as an ordained Seventh-day Adventist minister.

One fruit of the contact with the European Adventists was the development of a missionary society at the 1869 General Conference session. "The object of this society," read the action, "shall be to send the truths of the third angel's message to foreign lands, and to distant parts of our own country, by means of missionaries, papers, books, tracts, etc." In introducing the society, James White claimed that the church received "almost daily applications to send publications to other lands" (RH, June 15, 1869).

By 1869 the need to eventually send missionaries to other nations had become a reality for many Seventh-day Adventists. The church more and more clearly understood the mission imperatives of Revelation 10:11 and 14:6.

The big year was 1874. In January the denomination established the *True Missionary*, Adventism's first mission journal. In September John Nevins Andrews sailed for Europe as the denomination's first "official" foreign missionary. That same year saw the establishment of Battle Creek College. The timing for the establishment of the college was not accidental, since the founders at their clear-thinking best realized that a major purpose of the college would be to train mission personnel for both the home and foreign fields.

Between 1874 and 1887 the denomination established its presence in many nations of Europe as well as in Australia and South Africa. But still its view of missions was shortsighted. At this stage Adventists believed that their purpose was to call other Christians (generally Protestants) out of their churches and into the third angel's message. As yet, Adventism had little or no vision of mission to the "heathen" or to the great Roman Catholic fields in the New World.

But even that lack of vision had its utility. If the shut-door period of Adventist missiology provided time for the building of a doctrinal base, the mission-to-the-Protestant-nations era gave the denomination opportunity to establish population and financial bases in strategic locations that it could later use for sending missionaries around the world. By 1890 the denomination was poised for mission "explosion" and expansion "to *every* nation, and kindred, and tongue, and people" (Rev. 14:6).

Other Important Developments Between 1863 and 1888

Before moving away from the 1863 to 1888 era, we should briefly look at three other events. The first is the beginning of Adventist efforts among the White population in the American South. The late 1870s saw the start of regular Adventist work in Virginia, Texas, and other Southern states, but for several reasons (including regional animosities and other post-Civil War difficulties), Adventism failed to find the ready reception and rapid growth that it had in the Far West.

A second Adventist milestone in the 1863 to 1888 era was the passing of two of the denomination's founders. Joseph Bates died on March 19, 1872, in the Western Health Reform Institute in Battle Creek, shortly before his eightieth birthday. The "old health reformer" had kept a strong program going until near the end. The year before his death he held at least 100 meetings besides those at his local church and the conferences that he attended.

On August 6, 1881, James White passed away at the age of 60, also in the Battle Creek Sanitarium. The Seventh-day Adventist Church would never have existed without his forceful leadership. White had literally burned himself out in building up the denomination.

A final point that we should note in the pre-1888 period was the growing agitation for a national Sunday law and the passage of many state Sunday laws. During the mid-1880s the local authorities arrested Adventists in such states as California and Arkansas for the crime of working on Sunday. This crisis led to the development and regular publication of the *American Sentinel of Religious Liberty* to combat the injustice. Beyond that, a great deal of prophetic excitement emerged in Adventist ranks. Things would get much more exciting by the summer of 1888.

For Those Who Would Like to Read More

Greenleaf, Floyd. *In Passion for the World: A History of Seventh-day Adventist Education*. Nampa, Idaho: Pacific Press, 2005. Pp. 15-40.

Knight, George R. *Ellen White's World: A Fascinating Look at the Times in Which She Lived*. Hagerstown, Md.: Review and Herald, 1998.

———. *Joseph Bates*. Pp. 44-57, 83-88, 158-162, 184-187, 199-202.

———, ed. *Early Adventist Educators*. Berrien Springs, Mich.: Andrews University Press, 1983. Pp. 1-94.

Maxwell, C. Mervyn. *Tell It to the World*. Pp. 152-173, 205-230.

Robinson, Dores Eugene. *The Story of Our Health Message*. Nashville: Southern Pub. Assn., 1955.

Schwarz, Richard W., and Floyd Greenleaf. *Light Bearers*. Pp. 100-145.

VandeVere, Emmett K. *The Wisdom Seekers*. Nashville: Southern Pub. Assn., 1972. Pp. 1-52.

White, Arthur L. *Ellen G. White*. Vol. 2, pp. 34-45, 73-127, 176-204, 297-311, 372-384.

CHAPTER 5

Era of Revival, Reform, and Expansion

(1888-1900)

By 1888 the Seventh-day Adventist Church had its doctrinal/prophetic platform in place, it had organized to facilitate its preaching of the three angels' messages, and it had developed a distinctive lifestyle. The denomination had become a unique religious body gradually spreading throughout the world.

It is only natural that it trumpeted its uniqueness—especially its pillar doctrines, including the premillennial return of Christ, His ministry in the heavenly sanctuary, conditional immortality, spiritual gifts, and the importance of the seventh-day Sabbath. The church perceived its mission to be that of converting other Christians to Adventism's precious message. With that aim in view, most Seventh-day Adventists ignored those aspects of Christianity that they already shared with other Christians. That neglect had developed to problem-causing proportions by the time of the 1888 General Conference session at Minneapolis, Minnesota.

The 1888 General Conference Session

The Minneapolis General Conference session was one of

the most explosive and significant meetings the denomination has ever had. In order to understand why, we need to look at the context in which it took place.

The 1880s were no normal decade in Adventism. Rather, they were a period that saw the United States progressively move toward a national Sunday law crisis. It had been developing since the 1860s, when such organizations as the National Reform Association came into being with the aim of keeping America Christian. A major plank in the association's platform was the desire to protect Sunday sacredness.

By the early 1880s some Americans had come to see Seventh-day Adventists as "problems" in the drive to protect "the Lord's day." The conflict began to heat up in 1882 when local California authorities arrested W. C. White, the youngest son of James and Ellen, for operating the Pacific Press on Sunday. By 1885 Adventists were being arrested in Arkansas, and by 1888 the problem had spread to Tennessee and other states. In the next few years some Adventist ministers served on chain gangs with common criminals. Their crime: Sunday desecration.

The high-water mark in the excitement on the Sunday issue came on May 21, 1888, when New Hampshire senator H. W. Blair introduced a bill into the United States Senate for the promotion of "the Lord's day" "as a day of religious worship." Blair's national Sunday bill was the first such legislation to go before Congress since the establishment of the Adventist movement in the 1840s.

Seventh-day Adventists did not miss the prophetic significance of the proposed Sunday legislation. It seemed obvious to them that the forming of the image to the beast of Revelation 13, the giving of the mark of the beast, and the end of the world loomed close at hand. Clearly it appeared that Adventist preaching for the past 40 years on the books of Daniel and the Revelation was about to be fulfilled. With that in mind, it is not difficult to see why some of the Adventist leaders reacted violently and emotionally when others of their number began to reexamine the validity of certain aspects of the denomination's interpretation of prophecy and its theology of the law. Such questioning, they reasoned, publicly threatened the very core of Adventist identity in a time of utmost crisis.

The problem arose when two young Adventist editors from California began to publish articles in *Signs of the Times* between 1884 and 1886 that contradicted the denomination's developing "tradition." A. T. Jones, an aggressive student of prophecy, came up with a new interpretation for one of the ten horns of Daniel 7. That did not sit well with Uriah Smith, longtime editor of the *Review and Herald* and the acknowledged authority on prophecy among Adventists.

About this same time E. J. Waggoner expressed in print the idea that the law in Galatians was the moral rather than the ceremonial law. George I. Butler, president of the General Conference, saw in Waggoner's move the seeds for the overthrow of the denomination's position on the perpetuity of the Ten Commandments.

Both issues took on frightful proportions in the context of the developing Sunday law crisis. It hardly looked like an auspicious time for Adventists to be publicly arguing over their prophetic interpretation and their theology of the law. The crisis grew between 1886 and 1888, coming to a head at the General Conference session in October and November of 1888. Unfortunately, given the emotionally laden atmosphere and the strong personalities of the participants, the conference turned out to be confrontational and somewhat less than Christian.

Ellen White supported the right of Jones and Waggoner to have a hearing despite the objections of Smith, Butler, and the majority of the delegates. She deplored the harsh, condemning attitude that the Smith-Butler faction displayed, calling it "the spirit of the Pharisees" and "the spirit of Minneapolis."

As the conference proceeded, Ellen White ever more clearly saw that the traditionalists lacked the love of Jesus in their hearts. They had thoroughly imbibed the distinctive Adventist doctrines of the law, the sanctuary, and so on, but they did not understand what it meant to be saved by the righteousness of Christ and sanctified by His softening love. She perceived that Smith, Butler, and their colleagues needed to hear more of the Christ-centered message that Waggoner had been preaching.

As a result, during the Minneapolis session she joined Waggoner and Jones in uplifting Jesus. "My *burden during the meeting*," she wrote a few weeks later, "*was to present Jesus and His love before my brethren*, for I saw marked evidences that many had not the spirit of Christ" (1888 Materials 216; italics supplied).

"*We want the truth as it is in Jesus*," she told the denomination's leaders during the Minneapolis session. "*I have seen that precious souls who would have embraced the truth [of Adventism] have been turned away from it because of the manner in which the truth has been handled, because Jesus was not in it. And this is what I have been pleading with you for all the time—we want Jesus*" (*ibid.* 153; italics supplied).

Certain Adventist writers in the twentieth century have claimed that the 1888 message of Jones and Waggoner was something uniquely Adventist. But the facts do not bear out their contention. To the contrary, two of the most influential 1888 participants repeatedly contradicted that assertion.

E. J. Waggoner, for example, penned, "I do not regard this view which I hold as a new idea. . . . It is not a new theory of doctrine." To accept his position, he argued, "would simply be a step nearer the faith of the great Reformers from the days of Paul to the days of Luther and Wesley. It would be a step closer to the heart of the Third Angel's Message" (*Gospel in Galatians*, p. 70).

Ellen White agreed with Waggoner on the lack of uniqueness in his message. On October 21, 1888, she told the assembled delegates: "The Lord desires us all to be learners in the school of Christ. . . . God is presenting to the minds of men divinely appointed [Jones and Waggoner] precious gems of truth, appropriate for our time. God has rescued these truths from the companionship of error, and has placed them in their proper framework. . . . Brethren, God has most precious light for His people. I call it not new light; but O, it is strangely new to many" (1888 Materials 139, 140).

About a month after the Minneapolis meetings, she again reflected on the topic. "Elder E. J. Waggoner," she wrote, "had the privilege granted him of speaking plainly and presenting his views upon justification by faith and the righteousness of Christ in relation to the law. This was no new light, but it was old light placed where it should be in the third angel's message" (*ibid.* 211).

The true significance of the 1888 message of Minneapolis, as both Waggoner and Ellen White pointed out in the above quotations, is that it united faith in Jesus to the third angel's message. Prior to 1888 the Adventists had understood two of the three parts of Revelation 14:12—the foundational text in Seventh-day Adventist self-understanding and one quoted in full under the title of every issue of the *Review* for almost a century.

In terms of Revelation 14:12, the Adventists had understood "here is the patience of the saints" as the faithfulness of Seventh-day Adventists in continuing to wait for the Second Coming while preaching a judgment-hour message in spite of the October 22, 1844, disappointment. They had recognized "here are they that keep the commandments of God" as the

Adventists' uplifting of the perpetuity of God's law, including the true Sabbath.

Those two parts of Revelation 14:12 related to the distinctively Adventist contributions to theology. Unfortunately, 40 years of preaching their unique doctrines had led to a neglect of those beliefs that Adventists shared with other Christians, such as salvation by grace through faith in Christ. The significance of Jones' and Waggoner's preaching at Minneapolis was that it reunited the distinctively Adventist truths with the all-important message of salvation in Christ alone. Thus in 1888 some Adventists began to understand more fully the third part of Revelation 14:12—"the faith of Jesus," which, suggested Ellen White, meant "Jesus becoming our sin-bearer that He might become our sin-pardoning Saviour" (*ibid.* 217).

That insight, naturally, unsettled those who had put their confidence in the law. During a ministers' meeting in early 1890, Ellen White had to face that problem. She pleaded with the assembled ministers to go from the convocation with the message of Christ's righteousness so much a part of them that they could not hold their peace. But if they did, she told them that "men will say, 'You are too excited; you are making too much of this matter, and you do not think enough of the law; now, you must think more of the law; don't be all the time reaching for this righteousness of Christ, but build up the law.'"

To such "good" Adventist sentiments she replied, "*Let the law take care of itself. We have been at work on the law until we get as dry as the hills of [G]ilboa. . . . Let us trust in the merits of Jesus. . . .* May God help us that our eyes may be anointed with eyesalve, that we may see" (*ibid.* 557; italics supplied).

The significance of the 1888 meetings is that they baptized Adventism anew in Christianity. Adventists—at least some of them—finally understood the entire third angel's message. From that point on, they could preach a full message that taught the distinctively Adventist doctrines within the context of the saving work of Christ.

At last Seventh-day Adventists had the complete message of the third angel that they needed to preach "to every nation, and kindred, and tongue, and people" before the great Second Advent harvest of Revelation 14. The next decade saw Adventism not only grow in its understanding of vital Christian truth but also expand worldwide as the denomination finally grasped the extent of its missionary task.

The Aftermath of Minneapolis

Jones' and Waggoner's Christ-centered message received a mixed response among the participants at the conference. Some of the Adventist leadership accepted it, but most rejected both the men and their message. W. C. White noted shortly after the conference that the delegates returned home with "a great variety of sentiments. Some felt that it had been the greatest blessing of their lives; others, that it marked the beginning of a period of darkness" (WCW to J. N. Loughborough, Nov. 20, 1888).

Immediately after the Minneapolis meetings, Jones, Waggoner, and Ellen White began a sustained campaign to take their message to the Adventist people. Up through the fall of 1891 the three toured the United States, preaching righteousness by faith to the people and the ministers. After Mrs. White left for Australia in 1891 and Waggoner had gone to England, Jones and W. W. Prescott continued to champion the cause in North America. All through this period and beyond it, Ellen White emphasized that God had chosen Jones and Waggoner to bear a special message to the Adventist Church.

George I. Butler resigned as General Conference president in November 1888 in protest against the support given to Jones and Waggoner. On the other hand, Butler's successors in the presidential office—O. A. Olsen (1888-1897) and George A. Irwin (1897-1901)—responded positively to the young reformers and gave them broad exposure throughout the 1890s. They had access to the people through the churches, the Sabbath school lessons, the colleges, the in-service schools regularly held for the ministry, and the denomination's publishing houses.

Especially important was the fact that during every General Conference session from 1889 through 1897, Jones and Waggoner received the leading teaching role as they preached their message to the delegates in scores of sermons. Beyond that, by 1897 the denomination had made Jones the editor of the *Review and Herald.* As the denomination's most influential editor, he used the *Review* as a channel for his teachings. It would be hard to conceive of a program that could have given the reformers more prominence during the 1890s.

We should also note that the Christ-centered emphasis at Minneapolis created a definite shift in Mrs. White's literary production. Realizing more fully than ever the hardness and barrenness of a church overemphasizing mere doctrine, she began to stress the loving character of Jesus and His righteousness. The post-1888 years saw such Christ-centered books as *Steps to Christ* (1892), *Thoughts From the Mount of Blessing* (1896), *The Desire of Ages* (1898), *Christ's Object Lessons* (1900), and the opening chapters of *The Ministry of Healing* (1905) flow from her pen.

One of the unfortunate aspects of Adventist history is that some believers in the 1890s interpreted Ellen White's enthusiastic support of Jones and Waggoner as a kind of theological blank check—especially in issues involving righteousness by faith. As a result, by late 1892 some began treating Jones as a kind of prophetic extension of Ellen White.

From the Minneapolis conference onward she had to fight that mentality. During the 1888 meetings she flatly asserted that "some interpretations of Scripture given by Dr. Waggoner I do not regard as correct." Again in 1890 she had to tell a group of ministers that the two reformers were not "infallible" (1888 Materials 164, 566).

Unfortunately, some at that meeting and others a century later have had a hard time internalizing her cautions regarding the 1888 reformers. The human temptation is always to rely on people, when the obvious message of Ellen White, Jones, and Waggoner at Minneapolis was to get back to the Bible for religious authority and to the Christ of the Bible for salvation.

The post-1888 years also saw continuing agitation in the arena of state and national Sunday legislation. In the early 1890s the case of R. M. King, sentenced to prison for the crime of "hoeing in his potato patch on Sunday," was scheduled to go before the United States Supreme Court (D. T. Jones to A. T. Jones, June 25, 1890). But King died in November 1891, and the hearing was canceled.

Because of the Sunday agitation, the 1890s was a decade of great prophetic excitement among Seventh-day Adventists. Beyond that, it was a time in which they continued to strengthen their religious liberty activities.

Spiritual Revival and Educational Expansion

One of the most remarkable developments stimulated by the Christ-centered emphasis of the 1888 General Conference session was the reorientation and expansion of Adventist education. As of 1890 the denomination had established only 16 schools, including elementary schools, secondary schools, and colleges. However, by the end of the decade the church had 245 educational institutions at all levels. Progress was slow at first, but between 1895 and 1897 educational revival and expansion gained a momentum that continued through the Great Depression of the 1930s.

While 1891 saw the founding of Union College in Nebraska and 1892 witnessed the establishment of Walla Walla College in Washington, the real turning point in Adventist education took place at a convention in northern Michigan.

During the post-1888 period the General Conference held a number of ministerial institutes under the direction of W. W. Prescott, the leader of the Adventist educational program. The institutes sought to enlighten the denomination's clergy on the centrality of righteousness by faith to Adventism's theology and mission. Early in 1891 Prescott decided to provide a similar institute for Adventist educators. That crucial meeting took place at Harbor Springs, Michigan, during July and August 1891. Participants at the meeting describe it as a spiritual feast, with Jones preaching from the book of Romans and Ellen White speaking on such topics as the necessity of a personal relationship with Christ, the need for spiritual revival among Adventist educators, and the centrality of the Christian message to education.

Prescott proclaimed to the 1893 General Conference session that Harbor Springs had marked the turning point in Adventist education. Since that convention, he noted, the "religious element" had become central in Adventist schools. Whereas before Harbor Springs the Bible had held a marginal place in the curriculum of Adventist colleges, since the convention those same institutions had made significant progress in implementing the four-year Bible program recommended at that time. Even more important, "the Bible as a whole" was being studied "as the gospel of Christ from first to last," and teachers now presented Adventist doctrine in the context of the cross (1893 GCB 350).

The Christocentric revival in the denomination's theology had led to a spiritual revival in its educational program, accompanied by a clearer vision of educational purpose. As a direct result, Prescott claimed in 1893, "during the last two years there has been more growth in the educational work than in the seventeen years preceding that time" (*ibid.* 357).

Ellen White sailed for Australia three months after the close of the Harbor Springs meetings. She took with her a heightened awareness of the possibilities of Christian education and of the implications of the gospel for education.

During her years in Australia she had unequaled opportunity to influence the development of the Avondale School for Christian Workers along the lines of the principles enunciated at Harbor Springs. The Australian school, with its emphasis on the spiritual, its work-study program, its rural location, and its service orientation, developed into a model school under the direction of its reforming founders. By the turn of the century, the Avondale model was shaping Adventist schools around the world. Even Battle Creek and Healdsburg colleges sold their campuses and moved to rural locations in order to implement the Avondale ideals.

Out of the Avondale experience flowed a constant stream of letters and articles on Christian education from Ellen White's pen. Those writings not only guided the Christian development of existing Adventist schools, but also generated a pervasive atmosphere of awareness among Adventist leaders and members of the importance of Christian education.

Ellen White's counsel on elementary education during the midnineties was particularly important to the spread of Adventist education. Australia required school attendance. As a result, she suggested that Adventists should establish schools wherever there were "six children to attend" (6T 199).

Educational reformers in America read her counsel, including Edward Sutherland and Percy Magan (the president and dean, respectively, of Battle Creek College), who immediately began to push for the rapid development of an Adventist elementary system. Whereas the denomination in 1895 had 18 elementary schools worldwide, by the year 1900 the number had increased to 220, to 417 by 1905, and to 594 by 1910. Elementary education may have been a late development in Adventism, but once under way it appeared among Adventist congregations everywhere.

Minneapolis (with its emphasis on Christ's righteousness), Harbor Springs, Avondale, and the elementary school movement were not unrelated. Each led to the next, resulting in vigor and growth throughout the system.

Closely related to the revival and expansion of Adventist education was the parallel explosion in the number of Adventist missions in all parts of the world. Not only did the schools supply evangelistic and institutional personnel for the burgeoning mission enterprise, but the new missions soon established their own educational institutions. Thus, just as there was a direct relationship in 1874 between the sending of the first overseas missionary and the establishment of the first Adventist college, so a connection existed between the revival in Adventist education and missions in the 1890s. Adventist education has always been healthiest when tied closely to the denomination's mission.

Worldwide Mission Explosion

As we saw in previous chapters, Seventh-day Adventists were reluctant missionaries at best during the formative years of their movement, but by 1889 the denomination stood on the verge of a mission explosion throughout the world.

A series of firm foundations undergirded the rapid expansion. First, the "antimission" or shut-door period (1844-1850) of Adventist thinking had allowed for the development of a doctrinal base. Second, the partially opened-door period (1850-1874) provided time for building a power base in North

America that could support missions to other Protestant nations. And third, the mission-to-the-Protestant-nations period (1874-1889) provided for similar development in England, Europe, Australia, and South Africa. Even though much development still needed to take place in each of the mission home bases after 1890, the groundwork had been laid, and Adventism was ready to become a truly worldwide church in the 1890s.

The growing commitment of the denomination to foreign missions became ever more evident in the early and mid-1880s. One expression of that trend was a series of visits to the European mission by prominent Adventist leaders between 1882 and 1887. The first to go was S. N. Haskell, sent to Europe by the General Conference in 1882. Haskell recommended publishing in more languages, and he helped the Europeans to develop a more functional organizational structure.

More important, however, were the travels of General Conference president George I. Butler in 1884 and of Ellen White and her son W. C. White from 1885 through 1887. Such visits both strengthened Adventism in Europe and demonstrated the denomination's interest in missions.

By the middle of the 1880s the European Council had formed to guide Adventism in the "Old World." In addition, during that decade European Adventism produced publications in several more languages and took steps toward providing its own educational institutions to train church employees. Meanwhile, Adventists had begun work among European Protestants in Australia (1885) and South Africa (1887).

Perhaps one of the strongest signals that Adventism was beginning to enlarge its missiological vision took place in 1886. In that year the denomination published its first book on foreign missions—*Historical Sketches of the Foreign Missions of the Seventh-day Adventists*. Then in early 1889 the church sent Haskell and Percy T. Magan on a two-year itinerary around the world to survey opportunities, problems, and possible sites for Adventist missions in various parts of Africa, India, and eastern Asia. They fully reported their tour to the church through the pages of the *Youth's Instructor*. Thus missions and mission service began to capture the hearts and minds of Adventist youth.

It is important to note that Adventist young people were not the only ones being inspired toward mission service in the 1880s and 1890s. Protestant youth in the United States and elsewhere became interested in such service as never before. One factor was the Student Volunteer Movement for Foreign Missions, which grew out of an appeal by Dwight L. Moody in 1886 for college students to devote their lives to mission service. One hundred took their stand. That number increased to 2,200 in 1887, and within a few years many thousands of young people had pledged their lives to foreign missions. The movement's thrust was that "all should go to all," and its motto was "the evangelization of the world in this generation."

Similar awakenings took place among the young people of England, Scandinavia, Germany, France, Switzerland, and Holland. The 1890s were the great decade for Protestant missions. Adventism was prepared to participate in that enthusiasm and outreach.

Not only did contemporary mission excitement among other Protestants stimulate Adventism, but the 1888 meetings at Minneapolis enabled the denomination to understand more clearly both the meaning of the message of the third angel of Revelation 14 and the mission imperative included in it. Beyond that, the Sunday law crisis, viewed in the context of the message of the third angel, with its contrast between those who receive the mark of the beast and those who keep the commandments of God, gave Adventists a sense of urgency to carry their teachings throughout the world.

In November 1889 the General Conference session took

the momentous step of creating the Seventh-day Adventist Foreign Mission Board "for the management of the foreign mission work" of the denomination (1889 GCB 142). The same year saw the *Home Missionary* developed as a periodical aimed at promoting Adventism's various missionary enterprises.

The creating of the Foreign Mission Board was more than symbolic. It proclaimed that Adventists were at last ready to take the mission mandates of Revelation 14:6; 10:11; and Matthew 24:14 seriously. They would preach the three angels' messages—including both the great gospel truths recovered in 1888 and the distinctive Adventist doctrines—"to every nation, and kindred, and tongue, and people" that the end might come.

Never again were Seventh-day Adventists backward about foreign missions. To the contrary, they have become known for their efforts to reach the entire world with their message. In the process they have established publishing, medical, and educational institutions wherever they have gone.

By the end of the 1890s Adventism had established itself on every continent and in many island groups. In this period of Adventist missions the denomination aimed to reach the "heathen" and Roman Catholics as well as the world's Protestants. On the other hand, Adventist missionaries still usually began their work, in even non-Christian cultures, among the islands of Protestants in other nations. Such converted Protestants created an easily reached group that could form an indigenous base for further outreach.

Mission to Black America

A unique aspect of Adventist mission extension during the 1890s was an outreach to Black Americans. Although some Blacks participated in the Millerite movement (including Pastor William Foy, who filled a prophetic office from 1842 to 1844), early Sabbatarian Adventism was largely a White movement. In fact, it was roughly a half century after the Great Disappointment before Seventh-day Adventism got under way among North American Blacks with any real success.

It has been estimated that only about 50 Black Seventh-day Adventists existed in the United States in 1894, but by 1909 that number had climbed to 900. The growth in Black membership largely resulted from several mission projects aimed at evangelizing Blacks during the nineties.

The 1870s and 1880s witnessed sporadic work among Southern Blacks in Texas, Tennessee, Georgia, and other states, with the first Black congregation being officially organized at Edgefield Junction, Tennessee, in 1886. But White "Yankees" were somewhat at a loss as to how to face the peculiar racial problems of the South. They not only faced suspicion among Southern Whites for being Northerners, but were in a quandary on how to handle such issues as segregation.

Their work often met with violence from local Whites, who feared that the intruders might be preaching the "dangerous" doctrine of racial equality. Given the difficulties, the leadership finally concluded that it would be best to follow social convention by establishing separate congregations for the two races. Charles M. Kinney, the first African-American ordained as a Seventh-day Adventist minister, concurred with that decision. While Kinney did not see separate congregations as the ideal, he did believe that solution to be preferable to segregating Blacks to the back pews of White churches.

Kinney himself had been baptized into an integrated Adventist congregation in Reno, Nevada, in 1878. Recognizing his potential, the conference sponsored him at Healdsburg College from 1883 to 1885. Subsequently he worked as a colporteur in Kansas. Later he became pastor of the Edgefield Junction church in Tennessee, and he received ordination to the gospel ministry in 1889.

By 1891 Ellen White had become concerned over the lack of Adventist activity among American Blacks. On March 21 she presented a "testimony" on the topic to the delegates of the General Conference session. She especially called for more work among Southern Blacks. Her appeal soon went into print as a 16-page tract entitled *Our Duty to the Colored People.*

But the church neglected both the tract and its message until 1893, when James Edson White "discovered" the document. Edson, Ellen's oldest living son, had recently experienced conversion in his mid-40s. In his zeal he became convicted that he should take the Adventist message to the Blacks of the Deep South.

The ever-creative Edson soon linked up with Will Palmer (another recent convert with a dubious background) to build a "mission boat" and to enter into one of the most exciting chapters in North American Adventist missions. The two unlikely missionaries built the *Morning Star* in Allegan, Michigan, in 1894 at a cost of $3,700. Their vessel eventually served as a residence for the Adventist staff. In addition, it provided space for a chapel, library, printshop, kitchen, and photography lab.

White and Palmer floated their "mission station" across Lake Michigan and down the Mississippi River to Vicksburg, Mississippi, where they set up headquarters. Not having the confidence of the Adventist Church leaders, White and his colleagues were largely self-supporting in their mission endeavor. One project they used to raise money was the publication of the *Gospel Primer*, a book that was simple enough to use in teaching illiterates to read and that conveyed Bible truth in the process. The sale of that successful little volume helped finance the mission.

From Vicksburg the work spread to the surrounding countryside, often in the face of White resistance and violence. By the early years of the twentieth century the mission had nearly

50 schools in operation. In 1895 Edson's self-supporting mission organized as the Southern Missionary Society. In 1901 the society became a part of the newly established Southern Union Conference. Eventually the publishing arm of the enterprise also came under denominational ownership as the Southern Publishing Association, headquartered in Nashville, Tennessee.

The mid-1890s also saw the establishment of a training school for Black workers. The General Conference opened Oakwood Industrial School in 1896 on a 360-acre plantation near Huntsville, Alabama. The "industrial" in the title reflected the move by the denomination to make education more practical and thus bring it into line with the reform ideals set forth in Ellen White's "Proper Education" in 1872. Adventists established several secondary schools with "industrial" in their names during the 1890s, including Keene Industrial Academy in Texas and Woodland Industrial School in Wisconsin. In part, these schools modeled themselves after the then-developing Avondale Adventist school in Australia. The school established for ex-slaves by Booker T. Washington at Tuskegee, Alabama, provided another role model.

Oakwood soon became the center for training Black leadership. In 1917 it became Oakwood Junior College, and in 1945 granted its first baccalaurate degrees. It is currently a fully accredited university offering graduate programs.

The Contribution of Female Ministers in Early Adventism

Because the bulk of Adventism's ministry has consistently been male, too few have recognized the contribution to the church made by women who have served as ministers and in other official positions. The role of Ellen White, of course, was central to the establishment and development of Adventism. Even though the denomination never formally ordained her, as early as 1872 it listed her as an ordained minister, apparently so that she could receive a full ministerial salary. Believing that her ordination came from God, she does not appear to have been concerned about the human laying on of hands. What is beyond doubt, however, is that she was probably the most influential "minister" ever to serve the Adventist Church.

Many other women participated during the late nineteenth and early twentieth centuries as licensed ministers. One of the first may have been Sarah Lindsay, licensed in 1872. The denominational yearbooks list more than 20 additional women as being licensed ministers between 1884 and 1904—the first 20 years of the publication of the yearbook.

In spite of the fact that those women faced discrimination at times, they often made major contributions to the church. Minnie Sype, for example, established at least 10 churches. Beyond her evangelistic work, she performed such ministerial tasks as baptizing, marrying, and conducting funerals.

Lulu Wightman was one of Adventism's most successful and powerful female evangelists. Being credited with starting at least 17 churches, she far outdistanced most of her male contemporaries.

Later, Jessie Weiss Curtis presented 80 converts for baptism at the conclusion of her first evangelistic campaign. The Drums, Pennsylvania, church originated in that effort. She extended her influence by training ministerial interns for the conference. One of those was N. R. Dower, who later became the director of the General Conference Ministerial Department.

Although periodic talk of ordaining these and other women to ministry would surface, the church took no formal action in that direction. The 1881 General Conference session, however, did resolve "that females possessing the necessary qualifications to fill that position, may, with perfect propriety, be set apart by ordination to the work of the Christian ministry." Although referred to the General Conference Committee, the resolution never came to a vote (RH, Dec. 20, 1881).

In addition to those women who held ministerial credentials, many others served the denomination in various ways. Most, of course, had traditional female roles as teachers and nurses, but others held less traditional positions. Among them were L. Flora Plummer, who became secretary of the Iowa Conference in 1897 and served as acting conference president for part of 1900. In 1901 she became the corresponding secretary for the newly organized General Conference Sabbath School Department. And in 1913 she became the department's director, a position she held for the next 23 years.

Anna Knight also filled a unique position in Adventism. In addition to her pioneering educational work among Southern Blacks, she had the distinction of being the first African-American woman missionary sent to India from America.

Scores of other Adventist women in the late nineteenth and early twentieth centuries served in such elected offices as conference treasurers, conference secretaries, educational department leaders, and Sabbath school department leaders.

Too often we have overlooked the contributions of women to the development of Adventism. Both their potential and the problems they face resurfaced in the 1970s and 1980s. We will return to that topic in our final chapter.

The turn of the century found Adventism growing both in the United States and around the world. Along with the rapid expansion of missions in the 1890s, the denomination also had established medical, publishing, and educational institutions wherever it went. The beginning of the new century found the adolescent church overextended both financially and organizationally. Thus the twentieth century began in crisis.

For Those Who Would Like to Read More

Graybill, Ronald D. *E. G. White and Church Race Relations*. Washington, D.C.: Review and Herald, 1970.

———. *Mission to Black America*. Mountain View, Calif.: Pacific Press, 1971.

Greenleaf, Floyd. *In Passion for the World*. Pp. 40-103.

Habada, Patricia A., and Rebecca Frost Brillhart, eds. *The Welcome Table: Setting a Place for Ordained Women*. Langley Park, Md.: TEAM Press, 1995. Pp. 27-59.

Knight, George R. *A. T. Jones: Point Man on Adventism's Charismatic Frontier*. Hagerstown, Md.: Review and Herald, 2011. Pp. 17-165.

———, ed. *Early Adventist Educators*. Pp. 32-44, 115-183, 220-238.

———. *If I Were the Devil: Contemporary Challenges Facing Adventism*. Hagerstown, Md.: Review and Herald, 2007. Pp. 111-159, 201-209.

———. *A Search for Identity*. Pp. 90-127.

———. *A User-friendly Guide to the 1888 Message*. Hagerstown, Md.: Review and Herald, 1998.

Land, Gary, ed. *Adventism in America*. Pp. 77-96.

Olson, A. V. *Thirteen Crisis Years*: 1888-1901. Washington, D.C.: Review and Herald, 1981.

Reynolds, Louis B. *We Have Tomorrow: The Story of American Seventh-day Adventists With an African Heritage*. Washington, D.C.: Review and Herald, 1984.

Schwarz, Richard W., and Floyd Greenleaf. *Light Bearers*. Pp. 175-258.

Valentine, Gilbert M. *W. W. Prescott: Forgotten Giant of Adventism's Second Generation*. Hagerstown, Md.: Review and Herald, 2005. Pp. 47-144.

VandeVere, Emmett K. *The Wisdom Seekers*. Pp. 68-91.

Vyhmeister, Nancy, ed. *Women in Ministry: Biblical and Historical Perspectives*. Berrien Springs, Mich.: Andrews University Press, 1998. Pp. 187-234.

Whidden, Woodrow W. *E. J. Waggoner: From the Physician of Good News to the Agent of Division*. Hagerstown, Md.: Review and Herald, 2008.

White, Arthur L. *Ellen G. White*. Vol. 3, pp. 385-433, 448-462; vol. 4, pp. 42-47, 146-161, 287-314.

CHAPTER 6

Era of Reorganization and Crisis

(1900-1910)

By the beginning of the twentieth century the pattern of Adventism had been fixed. It had its doctrines fairly well hammered out, a distinctive lifestyle, and a worldwide mission program with extensive institutional support; and the denomination had even gone through a major period of revival and reform.

But all was not well as the church entered the new century. It had outgrown its 1863 organization. While that organizational structure had been adequate for a small North American movement with few employees and institutions, it was no longer functional for an increasingly complex denomination.

Thus the years of reform were not yet over. This time, however, the reforms were not doctrinal, as in 1888, but structural. Unfortunately, organizational reform in the early 1900s encountered just as much resistance as had doctrinal revitalization in the late 1800s. Change comes hard to those happy with the status quo, even when the change is imperative. Leaders with vested interests especially resist change.

So the church not only witnessed another round of reform

in the new century; it also endured a second crisis of personalities. By 1910, however, Seventh-day Adventism found itself reorganized and better fitted to accomplish its worldwide mission than at any time up to that point in its history.

Denominational Reorganization

The year 1901 was pivotal in Adventist history. At the 1901 and 1903 General Conference sessions the denomination thoroughly reorganized to conduct its mission more effectively.

A major difficulty with the 1863 organization was that it had centralized authority too much in the General Conference president. During the 1860s and 1870s the president was able to give careful attention to the work of the church in a quite personal manner. But between 1863 and 1901 the evangelistic force of the church jumped from 30 to about 1,500. Meanwhile, the number of local conferences had grown from six to nearly 100 (57 conferences and 42 missions). During that same period the Adventist membership had expanded from 3,500 to more than 78,000, representing about 2,000 local congregations.

A second problem with the 1863 organizational structure was its lack of unity. For example, the Sabbath school, publishing, medical, and other branches of denominational outreach operated independently of the General Conference. That caused real problems. One illustration of the difficulty is that the General Conference, the Foreign Mission Board, and the Medical Missionary and Benevolent Association each sent out missionaries without consulting the others. Beyond that, lack of unity permitted unbalanced growth in the denomination's programs. The medical organization, for example, employed more workers than all the other branches of the denomination combined—some 2,000 for the medical program as opposed to about 1,500 in the other areas.

Another difficulty was that the General Conference had inadequate financial control over other denominational entities. As a result, debt loomed at every hand in the medical, publishing, and educational branches. The church was in trouble, and it would take more than fine-tuning to solve the problem.

In summary, the task of reorganization involved both decentralization *and* centralization. On the one hand, presidential administrative authority needed to be dispersed. But on the other hand, the General Conference required more direct authority over its various branches.

The church had sensed the need for organizational change for some time. In fact, the 1880s and 1890s saw several successful experiments. A first step in the dispersal of administrative authority had actually taken place in 1882, when the denomination established the European Council of Seventh-day Adventist Missions to coordinate the work in Great Britain and Europe. A second, rather tentative, move came between 1888 and 1893, when the church divided its world work into eight districts. Those districts, however, lacked supervisory and administrative authority.

More substantial and lasting innovations took place in South Africa and Australia. In the early 1890s A. T. Robinson organized the Adventist work in South Africa along departmental lines. Instead of the Sabbath school and publishing programs being located in autonomous associations, they became integral parts of the conference. Thus the conference had a Sabbath school secretary, publishing secretary, and so on for each department. Each departmental secretary worked under the direction of the conference president. That development pointed the denomination toward a resolution of the problem posed by the decentralization aspect of its organizational difficulty.

W. C. White and another administrator from America by the name of Arthur G. Daniells adopted the "South African solution" for the Australian field in 1897. Meanwhile, Australia was making its own contribution toward solving the overcentralization-of-authority aspect of Adventism's organizational problem. It involved the formation in 1894 of an intermediate level of conference administration between the local conference and the General Conference—the union conference. Unlike the district system, the new union conference had administrative authority and administrative officers.

Beginning in 1897 the Australasian Union Conference also had a full set of departmental secretaries, a system soon duplicated in each of the local conferences in the union. Thus by the end of the nineteenth century the Australian church, under the leadership of Daniells, had a model that met the dual problems of centralization and decentralization that were plaguing Adventism's effectiveness. That model played a large role at the 1901 General Conference session.

In 1900 an aging Ellen White returned to the United States after nearly a decade in Australia. She encountered a church facing both theological aberrations and organizational overload.

There were two major theological aberrations. The first centered on tendencies toward pantheism among some of the church's leading theologians and the powerful John Harvey Kellogg. The second involved a strained view of perfectionism, as expressed in such movements as the holy flesh excitement that broke out in Indiana in 1900. The leadership put the holy flesh movement down rather quickly, even though more subtle forms of perfectionism lived on. But the pantheistic crisis became entangled with the move to reorganize. The upshot was the most significant schism (division) in the history of Seventh-day Adventism. We will return to the schismatic issues after we complete our examination of reorganization.

By 1900 Ellen White was a seasoned veteran in church

work. Beyond that, she was still capable of exerting the same forceful leadership that she had demonstrated in connection with her husband and Bates in the founding and organizing of Adventism. The 1901 General Conference session found her just as active in the reorganization as she had been in the drive for initial organization 38 years before. On the day before the opening of the session, Mrs. White met with a group of leaders in the library of Battle Creek College. In no uncertain terms she called for "new blood" and "an entire new organization" (MS 43a, 1901).

The first day of the session she again made her plea for reorganization, specifically speaking out against those who desired to wield "kingly power" (1901 GCB 26). Her plea led A. G. Daniells to move that the conference set its regular business aside and make reorganization the major agenda item. The session adopted his motion. Beyond that, it appointed the assertive young administrator (Daniells was 42 at the time) to lead the reorganization discussions. Neither he nor W. C. White (who had worked closely with Daniells in Australia) forgot the lessons they had learned in developing the union conference and departmental systems in the 1890s.

Given the prominent role of Daniells and W. C. White in the process of reorganization, it is not surprising that the 1901 General Conference session adopted both union conferences and departments. The result was that the "Australian solution" became the pattern for Adventist Church organization. With one major modification, this structure still exists as the church moves through the twenty-first century. The modification was the addition, between 1913 and 1918, of a fourth administrative level—divisions of the General Conference. The president of each "division" is also a vice president of the General Conference. By 1918 we could picture the administrative structure of Adventism as follows:

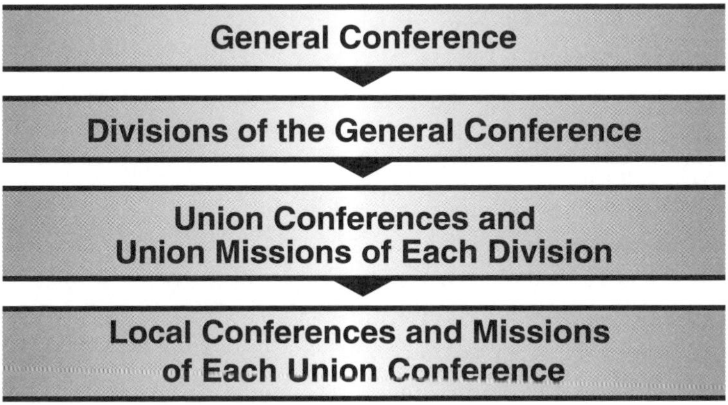

In summary, the 1901 General Conference session did much to solve both the overcentralization and decentralization tensions in the Adventist organizational structure. It had not only established an intermediate level of administration to supervise the work of local conferences in various parts of the world, but also adopted the departmental system to unify and coordinate the denomination's efforts. The departmental structure was duplicated at every level of Adventist organization, including that of the local church. Thus, for example, the religious liberty program had a person responsible for that aspect of Adventist concern at the General Conference and in each of its divisions, in each union and local conference, and in each local congregation.

Tension in the Power Structure

Unfortunately, there was a major exception to the departmental organization scheme adopted in 1901. One main segment of Adventism still remained independent: the Medical Missionary and Benevolent Association, presided over by the powerful and strong-willed John Harvey Kellogg.

In addition to being elated at his continued independence,

the assertive Dr. Kellogg also appreciated the fact that the General Conference had been greatly weakened in that it no longer had a president. Under the persistent argumentation of A. T. Jones, W. W. Prescott, and others, the 1901 session had voted that an Executive Committee would run the General Conference.

The doctor must have been even happier yet when the delegates decided to give his medical organization nearly one quarter of the votes on the Executive Committee. Those votes, when combined with those of his friends, meant that Kellogg not only might be able to remain independent himself, but also might be able largely to control General Conference decisions.

However, the equally forceful chair of the General Conference Executive Committee—A. G. Daniells—soon put to rest any aims Kellogg might have had along such lines. In Daniells, Kellogg met his match. For a time it had appeared that the doctor might be able to control the younger man, but by the middle of 1902 that illusion had shattered.

The primary bone of contention between Daniells and Kellogg was financial. The doctor had been quite used to doing things his way without much interference. That changed in 1902.

We can trace one aspect of the developing denominational crisis to February 18, 1902, when the massive Battle Creek Sanitarium burned to the ground. The rebuilding of the sanitarium soon created problems. The General Conference leaders, backed by Ellen White, wanted a modest reconstruction program, whereas Kellogg schemed from the start to erect a grander institution than its predecessor. In a church already burdened by debt, the issue became a constant irritant.

Even more immediately explosive, however, was the conflict between Kellogg and Daniells over the building of a sanitarium in Great Britain. Both men wanted the institution established, but Daniells insisted that it not involve deficit spending. All new enterprises, he held, must be on a pay-as-you-go basis. The confrontation infuriated Kellogg, who had been used to getting his way with the two previous General Conference administrators.

The solution, Kellogg quickly realized, was to replace Daniells with a General Conference Executive Committee chair more in harmony with his plans. That could be done easily enough, since the chair had no stated term of office and Kellogg had a powerful voting block and sympathy among the other committee members.

November 1902 saw the Kellogg forces make a drive to elect A. T. Jones to replace Daniells as chair of the denomination's Executive Committee. Daniells rose to the occasion, declaring, "*I'm* not a foot-ball: to be kicked into the ring, and then kicked out again" (AS, July 1922). After a stiff contest, the doctor's coup d'état failed, but its meaning was not lost on Jones. He dated that month as the exact time that he made his decision to cast his lot with Kellogg.

Meanwhile, Daniells, for reasons of daily business, assumed the title of "president" in his leadership of the Executive Committee. In the spring of 1902 W. W. Prescott, having been "converted" to Daniells' side of the struggle, was elected vice president.

Thus by the time of the 1903 General Conference session the sides in the power struggle had hardened, with Daniells and Prescott opposing Kellogg and Jones. Both factions approached the meetings with foreboding. Prescott alleged that there would be "a combining of . . . interests to make Brother A. T. Jones president of the General Conference" (W. W. Prescott to A. G. Daniells, Nov. 26, 1903). And Kellogg reported, "I have no hope for the future of this work unless the Daniells-Evans-Prescott ring can be broken up" (J. H. Kellogg to WCW, Mar. 18, 1903). All parties went into the 1903 session in a spirit of war.

After massive debates the 1903 session voted to modify the denominational structure in two ways that eventually spelled schism for the leaders of the Kellogg faction. The first change involved the reinstatement of the office of president. That was bad enough from the Kellogg-Jones perspective, but the delegates added insult to injury when they elected Daniells to the position.

The second change was even more devastating to the doctor. All denominationally operated institutions were to be placed under direct denominational ownership. Kellogg defiantly vowed before the delegates that he would never accept such a regulation.

His theological aberrations also complicated and intensified his struggle with the denomination's new leadership. For some years he had been enamored with pantheistically related ideas that made God a force within, rather than above, nature. Thus he could write: "There is present in the tree a power which creates and maintains it, a tree-maker in the tree, a flower-maker in the flower" (*The Living Temple*, p. 29).

But Kellogg was not alone in that perspective. One of the denomination's leading theologians, E. J. Waggoner of 1888 prominence, taught at the 1897 General Conference session that "God spake, and, lo! That Word [Christ] appeared as a tree, or as grass" (1897 GCB 34). At the 1899 session Waggoner claimed that "a man may get righteousness in bathing, when he knows where the water comes from" (1899 GCB 80).

The pantheism crisis came to a head in the context of the 1901 to 1903 power struggle between Kellogg and the denomination. Kellogg's publication of *The Living Temple* in 1903 especially stimulated it.

In writing the book, the doctor followed the lead of Ellen White, who had donated to the denomination the income from her newly published *Christ's Object Lessons*. The purpose of the donation was to pay off the large debt generated by the rapid expansion of the church's educational system. Kellogg, in like manner, intended to donate the profits of his book toward the rebuilding of the Battle Creek Sanitarium. Unfortunately for the doctor, Daniells, Prescott, and others decried *The Living Temple*'s pantheistic sentiments as an additional sign that Kellogg was untrustworthy.

The battle between Kellogg and his colleagues with the Daniells faction lasted for several years. Ellen White tried for some time to bring peace, but by 1903 she increasingly sided in public and in her writings with Daniells. Kellogg finally left the Adventist Church, being disfellowshipped from the Battle Creek congregation in November 1907. Siding with the doctor, and also leaving the church, were A. T. Jones and E. J. Waggoner—the two men who had pointed the denomination back to a fuller understanding of saving righteousness at Minneapolis in 1888. Jones fought against Adventism, church organization, and Ellen White for the rest of his life. On the Ellen White issue especially, Kellogg and several of his associates joined him between 1906 and 1910.

The Kellogg schism split several Adventist theologians and medical leaders away from the denomination. The doctor also managed to gain control of the rebuilt Battle Creek Sanitarium and the church's medical school—the American Medical Missionary College.

In addition to the schismatic crisis, Adventism faced other disasters at its Battle Creek home base. The year 1902 was particularly difficult. The sanitarium burned to the ground on February 18. A second fire followed on December 30 when the Seventh-day Adventist publishing house went up in flames. Within an hour it was a smoldering ruin despite the best efforts of the fire department.

The first years of the new century were some of the hardest for the denomination. Much that it had worked so hard to achieve had been destroyed. But all was not lost. Under the dynamic leadership of Daniells and Prescott, and with the continuing guidance of Ellen White, the very years that brought disaster also witnessed the rebuilding of Adventism on a stronger foundation than before.

In this section we have examined the strengthening of the denomination's organizational structure. In the next section we will look at Adventism's institutional rebirth.

The Battle Creek Exodus and New Beginnings

By the beginning of the twentieth century the continual migration of Adventists to Battle Creek had become a definite problem. Instead of living in various places where they could witness to their faith, a large portion of the Adventist membership had congregated in the city, gossiping among themselves and hindering the Adventist mission in other ways.

Beyond the large proportion of the denomination's membership in the city, Battle Creek had become overly centralized as the power base for world Adventism. Not only were the church's largest and most influential institutions located there, but also the world headquarters. A handful of men sitting on interlocking boards "ruled" Adventism everywhere. In fact, during the 1890s Battle Creek College, Battle Creek Sanitarium, and the Review and Herald Publishing Association took definite steps in the monopolistic spirit of the age to bring all other Adventist educational, medical, and publishing institutions around the world under their direct control.

In short, by 1900 Battle Creek had become to Adventism what Jerusalem was to the Jews and what Salt Lake City is to the Mormons. The new century, however, saw the breakup of Adventism's "holy city."

Ellen White had been urging it since the early 1890s. Not many, however, had responded. The first institutional leaders to advocate a move from the city were E. A. Sutherland and Percy T. Magan, president and dean, respectively, of Battle Creek College since 1897.

The two men had transformed the school from its classical orientation into a reform institution, with Bible, evangelism, and work-study programs at its center. In their zeal they also wanted to move the school out of Battle Creek as early as 1898. But Ellen White urged caution. By 1901, however, she and others recognized that the time had come. As a result, leadership decided to transfer the school to the sleepy little village of Berrien Springs in southwestern Michigan. There, with plenty of good land for agricultural and other industries, Sutherland and Magan founded Emmanuel Missionary College.

While the new school was quite a bit less than a college, it took the reform ideas even further than the reformers had done in Battle Creek. Sutherland's idea was to create "the Avondale of America" in Berrien Springs (P. T. Magan to EGW, July 14, 1901). The *missionary* in the institution's title indicated the purpose of the rechristened school. That word was rapidly becoming popular in the names of Adventist colleges. Beyond Adventism, the missionary college movement was a major arm of the drive among conservative American Protestants to evangelize the entire planet during the 1890s. Thus for both the Adventists and the evolving fundamentalists, the concept of colleges established for both practical and Bible-centered purposes had direct ties to their burden for foreign missions.

The college was not the only Adventist institution that departed Battle Creek in the early 1900s. The 1902 fire that destroyed the Review and Herald plant provided the necessary impetus to move both the publishing program and the General Conference headquarters out of the city. Where to go became the major issue for many. At first it appeared that New York City might be the appropriate location, but by 1903 Washington, D.C., had become the favored site.

The next few years saw the establishment of a new headquarters in Takoma Park, Maryland, just outside the Washington, D.C., boundary. Not only did the denominational leaders establish the General Conference headquarters and Review and Herald Publishing Association in Takoma Park, but a couple miles down the road they built the Washington Sanitarium and the Washington Training College. The latter institution they rechristened in 1907 as the Washington Foreign Missionary Seminary. Thus the new headquarters soon sported a full array of the typical Adventist institutions—a pattern that had come to mark Adventist outreach in every part of the world.

Takoma Park remained the headquarters for world Adventism for nearly nine decades. The Review and Herald Publishing Association eventually moved to Hagerstown, Maryland, in 1982-1983, and the offices of the General Conference transferred to Silver Spring, Maryland, in 1989. The sanitarium and college have remained at their original locations. The former is now known as Washington Adventist Hospital and the latter as Washington Adventist University.

The breakaway from Battle Creek brought with it a major shift in the Adventist medical program, and this time the forceful Kellogg was not in control.

The first aspect of the "new" Adventist medical work consisted of a new generation of Adventist sanitariums. The focal point of the medical program shifted from Michigan to southern California. Ellen White had begun pointing to California in 1902, even before the Kellogg difficulty reached a crisis level. God, she penned, "is preparing the way for our people to obtain possession, at little cost, of properties on which there are buildings that can be utilized in our work" (EGW to S. N. Haskell,

Sept. 27, 1902). Rather than one "mammoth institution" (7T 96), Ellen White counseled that the denomination should establish many smaller sanitariums in different locations.

The time was right for such a move. In the previous two decades entrepreneurs had built many health resorts in southern California's balmy climate. But hard times had hit the institutions, and many were up for sale at bargain prices. Ellen White, recognizing the opportunities, requested Dr. T. S. Whitelock and Pastor John A. Burden to keep their eyes open for suitable properties. That watching soon paid off.

In 1904 a group of Adventists under Mrs. White's leadership acquired what became the Paradise Valley Sanitarium at less than one sixth of the price of its construction some 15 years before. For eight years a group of Adventist ministers and laypeople operated the institution as a private venture. But they deeded it as a gift to the local conference when the conference became willing to accept responsibility for it in 1912.

The year 1905 witnessed the establishment of a second Adventist medical institution in southern California—the Glendale Sanitarium, near Los Angeles. And again Adventists, under the leadership of Burden and Ellen White, acquired the property at a fraction of its original cost.

Meanwhile, near Chicago, Dr. David Paulson opened the Hinsdale Sanitarium in 1905. Even though Paulson was still under the influence of Kellogg at that time, he remained loyal to the denomination both during and after the Battle Creek crisis.

However, the most important acquisition in the new Adventist medical work was the Loma Linda Sanitarium in southern California. Like the other California institutions, Adventists purchased it at a bargain price, and it began receiving patients in 1905, as did Hinsdale and Glendale.

The most significant thing about Loma Linda, however, was not its sanitarium, but the fact that it soon became the headquarters for the training of Adventist medical practitioners. As early as 1905 Ellen White had written that the denomination should train physicians at Loma Linda. But to many of the leaders of the Pacific Union Conference it seemed that such a program would take more money than they could raise. Furthermore, the times were inopportune for beginning a new medical school. During that very decade the American Medical Association initiated moves and standards that would force more than half of the medical schools in the United States to close permanently. Perhaps, some suggested, Mrs. White meant a Bible school that could instruct church workers in simple health treatments. Others held that she meant a fully equipped medical school that also taught Bible truths.

Complicating the issue was the fact that the only Adventist medical school at the time was under the control of John Harvey Kellogg, who had established the American Medical Missionary College at Battle Creek in 1895. But a decade later the Adventist leadership questioned the wisdom of placing students under Kellogg's influence.

To clear up the issue of what Ellen White meant by a medical education at Loma Linda, a group of Adventist leaders put the question to her in writing. She replied that "the medical school at Loma Linda is to be of the highest order." The denomination's young people, she said, should have access to "a medical education that will enable them to pass the examinations required by law of all who practise as regularly qualified physicians[;] we are to supply whatever may be required, so that these youth need not be compelled to go to medical schools conducted by men not of our faith" (PUR, Feb. 10, 1910).

The leaders responded positively to that counsel, even though they did not see how to accomplish it. The College of Medical Evangelists was incorporated on December 9, 1909. Today it is known as Loma Linda University.

In 1910 Kellogg's American Medical Missionary College closed its doors. The school's failure resulted partly from the dwindling supply of students as the doctor and the denomination distanced themselves from each other, and partly from rising standards for medical schools.

The Adventist medical program was not the only institutional sector of Adventism revitalized during the early years of the twentieth century. In chapter 5 we noted the beginning of reform and expansion in Adventist education. Those processes continued unabated throughout the first decade of the new century. While we do not have space to examine all of those changes in this chapter, it is important to take a quick look at one new educational development—that of Madison College.

Edward Sutherland and Percy Magan founded Madison College in 1904 in Madison, Tennessee. At the time it went under the name of the Nashville Agricultural and Normal Institute. The two reformers left their posts in Berrien Springs to establish a school that would train students as self-supporting missionary teachers. Their desire was to prepare young people who could not only preach the gospel but also instruct in health principles and better farming methods.

From its beginning the new school was unique in two ways. First, it aimed at being self-supporting in its operations (that is, it received no regular conference support); and second, it became a base for sending out additional self-supporting workers to new locations. The special sphere of Madison's influence was the American South, where the Adventist work still lagged behind that in most other parts of the nation. The school soon added a sanitarium to its facilities.

One of the most successful aspects of the Madison program was its reproduction across the South through the establishment of "units" in various localities. In their ideal form, the units replicated the Madison institution in new areas. Many of the Madison units later became conference schools and sanitariums as the conference structure in the South became stronger. Other units have remained as self-supporting institutions to the present day.

A Renewed Mission Emphasis

Before closing this chapter we should note one other aspect of Adventist activity during the 1901 to 1910 period: the continued expansion of and emphasis on Adventist mission to the world under the leadership of Daniells and William A. Spicer. It was the church's strong mission emphasis that finally led to reorganization and the creation of a new generation of institutions and the reformation of others.

Adventist missiology also gained a new emphasis between 1901 and 1910: large-city evangelism. Adventists were essentially a people of rural backgrounds. Thus it was not easy for them to adjust to dealing with the big cities. But that imperative became increasingly urgent in the face of escalating urbanization. The preaching of the three angels' messages "to every nation, and kindred, and tongue, and people" also meant evangelizing the cities, no matter how difficult or even distasteful that task might be. Once again, as with so many initiatives, Ellen White proved to be a moving force in urging the denomination forward.

Mission was central to Adventist thinking in the early years of the new century. By the end of its first decade Adventism was prepared to missionize the world with greater efficiency and balance than ever before.

For Those Who Would Like to Read More

Knight, George R. *A. T. Jones*. Pp. 166-284.

———. *Organizing for Mission and Growth*. Pp. 67-144.

Land, Gary, ed. *Adventism in America*. Pp. 96-112.

Era of Reorganization and Crisis

Moon, Jerry Allen. *W. C. White and Ellen G. White: The Relationship Between the Prophet and Her Son*. Berrien Springs, Mich.: Andrews University Press, 1993. Pp. 264-320.

Morgan, Douglas. *Lewis C. Sheafe: Apostle to Black America*. Hagerstown, Md.: Review and Herald, 2010.

Neufeld, Don F., ed. *Seventh-day Adventist Encyclopedia*. Vol. 10, pp. 173-179, 851-853; vol. 11, pp. 266-270.

Oliver, Barry David. *SDA Organizational Structure: Past, Present and Future*. Berrien Springs, Mich.: Andrews University Press, 1989.

Schwarz, Richard W. *John Harvey Kellogg, M.D.: Pioneering Health Reformer*. Hagerstown, Md.: Review and Herald, 2006

——— and Floyd Greenleaf. *Light Bearers*. Pp. 250-338.

Valentine, Gilbert M. *W. W. Prescott*. Pp. 145-213.

White, Arthur L. *Ellen G. White*. Vol. 5, pp. 70-110, 198-222, 243- 258, 271-306, 359-380; vol. 6, pp. 11-32, 270-290.

CHAPTER 7

Era of Worldwide Growth

(1910-1955)

The six decades from 1840 through 1900 saw the formation of Adventism as a world church. The decade of 1900 to 1910 witnessed the church reorganize its structures and institutions for a more functional fulfillment of its mission. And growth that would have been unimaginable to the Adventist pioneers has taken place since 1910. From a small and despised Advent band of about 100 in 1848, the church increased to approximately 78,000 in 1900. That figure was approaching the 18 million mark in mid-2012, and estimates based on current growth rates suggest that the church will have a membership of about 23 million by the year 2020. Also, whereas in 1900 the denomination was still predominantly North American, by the mid-1920s more than half its membership lived on other continents.

Early-twentieth-century Adventism might best be viewed as a people with a burning mission to take the three angels' messages to all the world. Between 1910 and 1955 the denomination had so strengthened and extended the mission program of the 1890s that the Adventism of the mid-1950s would have been almost unrecognizable to its founders.

The Passing of Ellen White

As we noted in our first few chapters, Ellen White, James White, and Joseph Bates were the founders of Seventh-day Adventism. Bates passed away in 1872 and James in 1881, but Ellen continued to guide the Adventist Church until 1915. Although she never held an official administrative position in the denomination, she possessed an immense charismatic authority. Her writings and counsels held special meaning for both individuals and corporate Adventism.

On July 16, 1915, "the little old woman with white hair, who always spoke so lovingly of Jesus" (in the words of some of her non-Adventist neighbors; see A. L. White, *Messenger to the Remnant*, p. 108) died at the age of 87. The last words that her family and friends heard were "I know in whom I have believed" (LS 449).

Three funeral services were held—one at Elmshaven, California, her home; a second at the Richmond, California, camp meeting; and the third at the Battle Creek Tabernacle. General Conference president A. G. Daniells directed the Battle Creek service. More than 3,500 persons filled the tabernacle, while 1,000 others were turned away for lack of room.

The end of Ellen White's life had come, but not her influence. By the time of her death her literary production consisted of more than 100,000 pages of books, tracts, periodical articles, and unpublished letters and manuscripts. Her written legacy to Adventism has continued to provide valuable counsel to the church to which she had dedicated her life.

Realizing that she would most likely die before the coming of Jesus, early in 1912 Mrs. White made provision for her writings in her last will and testament. She designated five men who at her death were to serve as a self-perpetuating board of trustees to handle her properties, "conducting the business thereof" and "securing the printing of new translations" and the "printing of compilations" from her manuscripts (the entire will appears in H. E. Douglass, *Messenger of the Lord*, pp. 569-571).

From 1915 until the present the trustees of the Ellen G. White Estate have performed these functions. In addition, they have acquainted both Adventists and others with Mrs. White and her work. The Ellen G. White Estate presently has its headquarters in the General Conference building in Silver Spring, Maryland. Branch offices and research centers connected with the White Estate exist throughout the world. Connected with leading Adventist educational institutions, these extensions of the White Estate's main office offer ongoing opportunities for research into Ellen White's writings and issues related to them.

A Period of Crisis and Promise

In spite of unprecedented world crises that included a crushing world depression, two world wars, and a cold war, between 1910 and 1955 the Adventist Church witnessed its largest growth and expansion up through that point in its history. While those crises hindered the preaching of the three angels' messages in some ways, in other ways the magnitude of the disasters heightened interest in the Second Advent. "Wars and rumors of wars" led people to take the "signs of the times" seriously. Periods of crisis have generally stimulated Adventist evangelism, even while hindering work in war-torn nations and frustrating communication across antagonistic international barriers.

The first half of the twentieth century brought not only the twin crises of war and economic depression but also a shift in the culture at large toward secularization. In many ways that cultural shift came to a climax in the years between World War I and the Great Depression of the 1930s. That was especially true in the United States, a nation that was at the time still the most influential fulcrum of world Adventism. During the 1920s events in North America tended to make a larger impression on the world church than do similar happenings in the first quarter of the twenty-first century.

Of particular importance to Adventism was the showdown between Protestant liberalism and fundamentalism. The core of the struggle between the liberals and the fundamentalists involved the nature of inspiration and revelation. Adventism at its best tended to follow the lead of Ellen White, who argued for thought inspiration rather than verbal inspiration and thus led Adventism away from ideas of inerrancy and infallibility. The Bible, she held, was infallible in the realm of salvation, but it was not infallible or inerrant in the radical sense of being beyond any possibility of factual difficulties or errors.

During the late nineteenth and early twentieth centuries such Adventist leaders as A. T. Jones and S. N. Haskell had caused serious problems in Adventism by teaching verbal inspiration and inerrancy for both the Bible and the writings of Ellen White. Mrs. White, however, was still alive and could speak for moderation on the topic. Allied with her were such Adventist leaders as A. G. Daniells and W. C. White, who continually pressed for a reasonable and not overly rigid view of the inspiration of the Bible and Ellen White's writings. Jones eventually rejected Ellen White because of her commonsense flexibility on inspiration—a position that conflicted with his doctrinaire rigidity.

Unfortunately, the force and magnitude of the struggles in American Protestantism during the 1920s destroyed the careful balance advocated by the Whites and Daniells. That decade saw polarization on the topics of verbalism and inerrancy between the fundamentalists and the liberals. While the liberals explained away the divinity of Scripture, the fundamentalists made their definitions so rigid that they are still warring over them nearly a century later.

Adventism found itself caught in the midst of the crisis over inspiration and, in the process, unfortunately, lost its balanced position. Events sidelined Daniells, Prescott, W. C. White, and other moderates on the topic of inspiration during the 1920s, as the church, in a fearful and reactionary mood, even went so far as to publish a General Conference-sponsored textbook for Adventist colleges that explicitly denied Ellen White's moderate position on thought inspiration and argued for inerrancy and the verbal inspiration of every word.

The loss of Ellen White's and Adventism's moderate stance on inspiration during the 1920s set the church up for decades of difficulties in interpreting the Bible and the writings of Ellen White. The resulting problems have led to extremism, misunderstandings, and bickering in Adventist ranks that exist, unfortunately, until the present.

On a more positive level, the 1920s saw a revival of interest in the righteousness of Christ and salvation in Him. Of special influence were such books as Daniells' *Christ Our Righteousness* (1926), Prescott's *Doctrine of Christ* (1920) and *Saviour of the World* (1929), Meade MacGuire's *His Cross and Mine* (1927) and *Life of Victory* (1924), and LeRoy Froom's *Coming of the Comforter* (1928).

Unparalleled Growth in Adventist Missions

For the first three decades of the twentieth century, two of the denomination's most mission-oriented leaders held its two top positions. A. G. Daniells served as General Conference president from 1901 to 1922, and then as General Conference secretary for the next four years. Meanwhile, William A. Spicer was secretary between 1903 and 1922 and president from 1922 to 1930. The presidential office in any organization is obviously important in setting directions, but in Adventism the secretariat is equally vital in terms of foreign missions, since that office took over the function of the denomination's Foreign Mission Board in 1903. Spicer and Daniells not only were able leaders, but also were dedicated to missions and the preaching of the third angel's message "to every nation, and kindred, and tongue, and people."

It is difficult to grasp the magnitude of the changes in Adventist mission outreach, but a graph indicating the increasing number of Adventist missions should help us gain some appreciation of an expansionary move that was beginning to transform the denomination from a North American church into a worldwide movement.

Figure 1

Expansion of SDA Missions

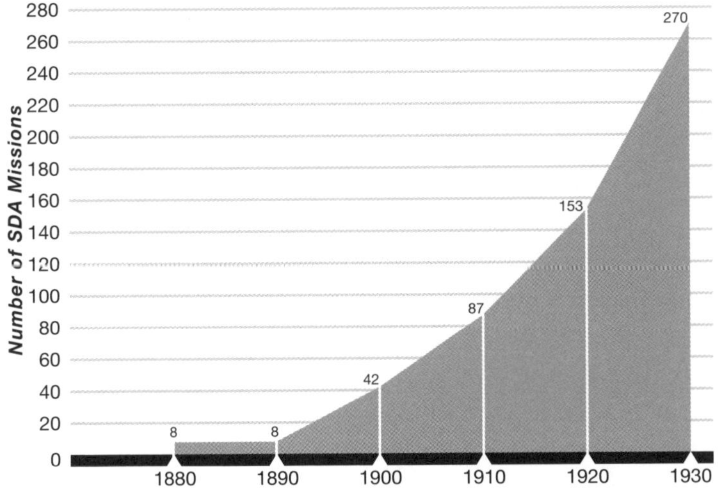

A glance at Figure 1 indicates several things. One is the lack of mission development before the 1890s. Second, as we noted in chapter 5, is the crucial importance of the 1890s as the decade in which Adventism came to understand its worldwide mission and then determined to carry out that mission.

The third thing to note is that this understanding and determination did not burn itself out in the 1890s. To the contrary, the expansion of the nineties continued unabated throughout the administrations of both Daniells and Spicer. And this continuous spread into all the world not only altered the geographical boundaries of the church but increasingly changed the nature of Adventism itself. Table 1 helps us come to grips with some important aspects of that transformation.

Table 1

Growth of SDA Church by Decades

Year	Evang. Workers North America	Evang. Workers Outside North America	Churches North America	Churches Outside North America	Membership North America	Membership Outside North America
1863	30	--	125	--	3,500	--
1870	72	--	179	--	5,440	40
1880	255	5	615	25	14,984	586
1890	355	56	930	86	27,031	2,680
1900	1,019	481	1,554	338	63,335	12,432
1910	2,326	2,020	1,917	852	66,294	38,232
1920	2,619	4,336	2,217	2,324	95,877	89,573
1930	2,509	8,479	2,227	4,514	120,560	193,693
1940	3,001	10,578	2,624	6,300	185,788	318,964
1950	5,588	12,371	2,878	7,359	250,939	505,773

An examination of Table 1 indicates not only continuous growth but also the fact that the 1890s and 1920s have particular interest. The 1890s, as we noted above, was the decade in which the church began to preach its judgment-hour messages as "a witness unto all nations." In the mid-1920s the denomination passed the point where it had more members outside of North America than inside. Thus the church not only preached worldwide but was beginning to become internationalized. That process continues as the church enters the twenty-first century. The full implications of the internationalization of Adventism, as we shall see in our final chapter, have yet to manifest themselves completely in a denomination that continues to be one of the fastest growing religious bodies in the world.

Some of the implications for internationalization were already becoming clear by the turn of the century. One was an expansion of home bases for sending out foreign missionaries. While that concept had begun during the nineteenth century, Daniells consciously sought to develop Adventism further in such nations as Germany, England, and Australia, in order to make them stronger home bases for additional expansion.

The early decades of the twentieth century witnessed the German church, under the leadership of Louis R. Conradi, pioneer Adventism in the Middle East and East Africa. Australian missionaries, meanwhile, rapidly spread the message throughout much of the South Pacific. British Adventism, with its nation's global empire and strongly developed missionary tradition, rapidly moved to plant Adventism in many parts of the world. As the century progressed, more and more missions in both developed and undeveloped nations became self-sustaining conferences that could function as home bases for additional mission outreach.

The generous giving of tithes and various mission offerings and the annual Ingathering campaign supported the denomination's ambitious outreach program. The church initiated "Harvest Ingathering" during the early 1900s to provide non-Adventists with an opportunity to assist Adventist projects.

Adventism, of course, took its medical, educational, and publishing work almost everywhere it went. The denomination's institutional base expanded in proportion to the spread of the church itself.

In many nations the Adventist door-to-door book salesperson—the colporteur—became the entering wedge for the three angels' messages. Adoption of innovative techniques in the fields of communication and transportation also facilitated the spread of Adventism.

In the mass publicity tradition of Joshua V. Himes, H.M.S. Richards envisioned the possibilities inherent in radio for spreading the Adventist message. In 1930 he began *The Tabernacle of the Air* on station KGER in Long Beach, California. Richards' program, renamed *The Voice of Prophecy*, later became one of the first religious programs to enter the national broadcasting field.

In a world in which TV was still a new and largely untried medium of communication, William Fagal's *Faith for Today* program first aired on May 21, 1950. The 1950s also saw George Vandeman begin the *It Is Written* telecast. The successes of Richards, Fagal, and Vandeman soon stimulated Adventists to use radio and television in other nations.

During the early 1990s the denomination developed powerful radio stations in various parts of the world with the idea of blanketing the planet with the three angels' messages. The late nineties saw the church move into such strategic areas of outreach as the Internet and the development of a worldwide satellite television communication network with downlink locations in thousands of locations. The full possibilities of, and results from, Adventist World Radio and creative uses of computer and satellite technology are yet to be seen.

Adventist missionaries were also eager to utilize advances in transportation. Of special interest is their missionary vessels. We have already noted J. E. White's innovative employment of the *Morning Star* in the American South in the mid-1890s, but an even more romantic venture had preceded it. In 1890 the denomination had launched the *Pitcairn* to spread the work among the islands of the South Pacific.

The most extensive use of Adventist missionary vessels, however, has undoubtedly been in the area of medical launches. In 1930, under the inspiration of Lower Amazon Mission president Leo B. Halliwell, the church constructed its first launch. The *Luzeiro*, christened in 1931, took medical care and the Adventist message to people living along the banks of the Amazon and its tributaries. The *Luzeiro* became the first of many such launches in Brazil and other nations. During the 1950s Adventists began to employ airplanes for similar purposes.

By the mid-1950s Adventism was truly a worldwide religious body. Its mission program had succeeded beyond expectation. The period also witnessed Adventist expansion in the United States among both the nation's majority and minority populations. It is to the significant growth among America's largest racial minority that we now turn.

The Maturation of Adventism Among African-Americans

An important North American "mission" that became increasingly integrated into Adventism throughout the twentieth century was the denomination's work among Americans with an African heritage. That process, however, was not speedy, nor were the results self-evident from the beginning.

Unfortunately, racial prejudice, like other sins, is not totally eradicated in most Christians at conversion. Nor are the racial tensions embedded in a culture easy for the churches existing in that social environment to overcome. Thus it is unfortunate, but not surprising, that Adventists had their share of casualties over racial issues as the number of Blacks increased in the denomination. One of the first was L. C. Sheafe. Sheafe rose to a degree of prominence in Adventist circles in the late 1890s, frequently speaking at General Conference sessions for much of the next decade.

By 1907, however, Sheafe, who was pastor of the People's Seventh-day Adventist Church in Washington, D.C., was in the process of leading his congregation out of the denomination. Part of the reason involved the issue of racial discrimination. Taking advantage of that situation, A. T. Jones came from Battle Creek to fan the flames of discontent. Subsequently, Sheafe, in league with Jones, sought to alienate Black churches in other parts of the country from the denomination.

Two years later, perhaps in response to the Sheafe defection, the General Conference established the North American Negro Department to look after the concerns of Black Adventists. The first three departmental secretaries, as we might expect, were Whites. That, however, changed in 1918 when a talented Black lawyer by the name of William H. Green became secretary, holding the position until his death in 1928. Under Green's leadership the work among African-Americans prospered in spite of continuing discrimination.

Discrimination, however, again prompted the defection of a leading Black pastor. In 1929 J. K. Humphrey led his 600-member First Harlem Seventh-day Adventist Church in New York City out of the denomination.

That same year found the most prominent Black pastors calling for Black conferences. A separate organization, they argued, would prosper the work among African-Americans. Most White leaders saw little light in that suggestion, and another decade and a half transpired before Black conferences became a reality. In the meantime George E. Peters and Frank L. Peterson headed the North American Negro Department.

The final drive for Black conferences took place in the early 1940s. In the lead were the highly educated members of the Ephesus Seventh-day Adventist Church in Washington, D.C. Located in close proximity to the denomination's world headquarters, the Washington members found it difficult to ignore their racially discriminated-against status in the church. They could not enroll their children at Washington Missionary College, nor could they eat in the cafeteria connected with the General Conference.

The crisis came to a head in the fall of 1943 when the Washington Adventist Sanitarium ordered that Lucy Byard, a light-skinned Adventist Black, be transferred to another facility after the hospital learned her racial identity. Because of a series of delays in moving her to the Freedmen's Hospital, she died of pneumonia. An incensed Black Adventist community saw Byard's death as a martyrdom to a policy of racial exclusiveness.

Subsequent events led to emotional discussions among Adventist leaders on how best to meet the needs of Black Adventists. The ideal for most Blacks was full equality in existing conferences. But denominational leaders in what was still a largely segregated culture were not willing to grant that desire. As a result, more and more of the denomination's leadership became convinced that Black conferences were the answer. In April 1944 the enabling act for the establishment of Black conferences occurred at the spring meeting of the General Conference. On January 1, 1945, the Lake Region Conference became the first Black conference in North America. Other "regional" conferences organized in quick succession.

Some Blacks had argued that Adventist work among minorities would be much more successful if carried on by people of the same race. The growth of Black Adventism since the establishment of Black conferences seems to amply support the concept. In 1944 Black membership stood at 17,000, 8 percent of the total North American Division membership. By mid-1997 Black membership had increased to 262,000, or 30 percent of the total. In other words, since work among North American Blacks came under their own control, the African-American sector of the church had grown nearly four times as fast as the rest of the division membership.

During the 1950s and 1960s North American Blacks increasingly held positions in the General Conference. That process undoubtedly speeded up under the influence of the civil rights movement in the larger culture during the early 1960s. In 1962 Frank L. Peterson became the first African-American vice president of the General Conference. The 1960s also saw the denomination go on record against racial discrimination in denominational institutions.

During the late 1960s and early 1970s a move surfaced to create Black union conferences in North America. In place of Black unions, however, it was eventually decided to give Black leaders more influence in the denomination through electing Black administrators to some of the offices in existing union conferences. Black representatives also received positions on committees. The same arrangements have been made with the growing Hispanic population in North America to ensure a Spanish American voice at all levels.

During the 1980s the denomination in North America witnessed Blacks in positions of leadership undreamed of in the 1950s or even the 1960s. Thus, for example, Charles E. Bradford was president of the North American Division, Robert H. Carter served as president of the Lake Union Conference, and Calvin Rock was a general vice president of the world church.

The question remains in some minds as to whether the church should have separate conferences on the basis of race. Calvin Rock points out that not all unions have separate conferences, and in those that do have them, they are not segregated. In fact, some regional conferences have White pastors, and "White" conferences have Black pastors and administrators. Rock's general argument is that regional conferences ought to remain an option if they facilitate the denomination's mission to the world (Adv. Rev., Sept. 26, 1991). On the other hand, as noted above, in many areas the "color line" is becoming more blurred in terms of both church attendance and leadership. That, of course, does not mean that the ideal has been reached or that all the tensions have disappeared.

With the ongoing internationalization of the church in the post-1955 period, the growth trends of world Adventism between 1910 and 1955 have continued. Church growth results similar to that among Black North Americans have been replicated around the world and in other minority groups in the United States, as Whites from North America, Europe, and other parts of the world increasingly have turned over leadership positions to indigenous staffs. If the first half of the twentieth century saw Adventism spread worldwide, the second half would witness it taking giant strides toward truly becoming an internationally integrated world religious body.

For Those Who Would Like to Read More

Greenleaf, Floyd. *In Passion for the World*. Pp. 104-352.

Knight, George R. *Meeting Ellen White*. Pp. 79-87.

———. *Organizing for Growth and Mission*. Pp. 145-151.

———. *A Search for Identity*. Pp. 128-159.

Land, Gary, ed. *Adventism in America*. Pp. 113-170.

Morgan, Douglas. *Lewis C. Sheafe*.

Reynolds, Louis B. *We Have Tomorrow*. Pp. 292-357.

Schwarz, Richard W., and Floyd Greenleaf. *Light Bearers*. Pp. 339-655.

Weeks, Howard B. *Adventist Evangelism in the Twentieth Century*. Washington, D.C.: Review and Herald, 1969. Pp. 11-245.

White, Arthur L. *Ellen G. White*. Vol. 6, pp. 302-448.

CHAPTER 8

The Challenges and Possibilities of Maturity

(1955-)

It is a well-known fact that individuals pass through a life cycle that begins in infancy, advances through rapidly developing adolescence and vigorous young adulthood, and progresses on into the slowing down of middle age. If a person lives long enough, he or she will eventually face the mental and/or physical decay of old age.

But it is less well recognized that organizations, including churches, pass through a similar aging process. Adventism has not escaped that dynamic. It passed through infancy between 1844 and 1863 and adolescence between 1863 and 1901. By 1901 it had reached, in sociological terms, the stage of maximum efficiency. Unfortunately, the stages beyond that level are no more pleasant for churches than they are for individuals. They are marked by institutionalism as an end in itself, bureaucracy, and eventually dysfunction.

However, the good news is that, unlike individuals, whose life cycle is biologically determined, social organizations do not necessarily have to pass into the degenerative parts of the cycle. The alternative is ongoing revival and reformation. For a church, that means two things: (1) always keeping its mission in view, and (2) maintaining a willingness to restructure and reform its organizations and institutions, thus keeping those entities functional in achieving the church's mission.

In chapter 6 we saw reform and restructuring taking place in the early 1900s as the denomination faced the challenges of being a world church with almost 80,000 members. Its previous organization and some of its institutions had become dysfunctional and unable to reach the church's primary goals in the most effective manner.

Adventism in 2012, with its almost 18 million members, stands at a similar crossroads. This chapter argues that Adventism reached denominational maturity in the mid-1950s and that after more than a half century of maturity the denomination needs consciously to reform and retool for renewed vigor. The alternative is to face the possibility of succumbing to the threats of institutionalism, secularization, and dysfunctionality. Such dilemmas are the lot of organizations that refuse to deal with the problems created by unusual success during their previous stages of development.

Adventism's prosperity and achievements during the early years of the twentieth century were outstanding. That success has continued up to the present, but it has brought the church to a place where it must consciously choose and courageously act, as it did in the 1860s and the first decade of the twentieth century, to transform itself for continued progress under changed conditions.

Adventism, as we will see, has developed aggressive new mission strategies, but the denomination also faces major challenges and problems. Fortunately, it has not only problems but also unprecedented possibilities if its leaders and members are willing to act with the dedication and singleness of vision that characterized the earlier leadership of the movement.

Arriving at Maturity

By the mid-1950s several signs were indicating that Seventh-day Adventism had matured as a denomination. One was the recognition by certain influential evangelical leaders that the church was indeed an evangelical Christian body.

Ever since the seeming failure of Millerism in the 1840s most Protestants had regarded Adventists with suspicion. The fact that they claimed a modern prophet in Ellen White and aggressively preached the perpetuity of the Ten Commandments, including the seventh-day Sabbath, aggravated the problem. Throughout the early twentieth century most Protestants considered Adventism a sect to avoid because of its heretical viewpoints. Many classed Adventists with Jehovah's Witnesses, Mormons, and Christian Scientists as being sub-Christian.

That perception changed in the mid-1950s as a result of a series of theological conferences between certain Adventist leaders and two prominent evangelicals. One was Donald Grey Barnhouse, the editor of *Eternity* magazine. The other was Walter Martin, a specialist on non-Christian cults commissioned by Zondervan Publishing House to write a book about Adventists.

Barnhouse and Martin concluded, to their own surprise, that Adventists did not believe in several heresies, including salvation by works, that others had attributed to them. While those evangelical scholars could not agree with every aspect of Adventist theology, they did conclude that Adventists were not sectarian. Rather, they were evangelical Christians who deserved to be recognized publicly as such.

As a result, Barnhouse extended the hand of fellowship to Adventism in the September 1956 issue of *Eternity*, and Martin wrote a favorable volume entitled *The Truth About Seventh-day Adventism* (1960). The denomination, meanwhile, published *Questions on Doctrine* (1957) as a reply to the queries of the evangelicals.

From that time forward Adventists have had a much better relationship with the larger Christian community. One unfortunate result of that recognition, however, has been a split in Adventist opinion over whether such recognition was a step forward in the church's distinctive mission or a step backward.

The development of denominational universities in the late 1950s and early 1960s offered a second sign of growing Adventist maturity. That move actually began in the early 1930s when the denomination finally accepted the fact that its college teachers would have to earn advanced degrees if the modern world was to accept graduates from Adventist colleges. That insight led to the establishment of the Advanced Bible School in 1934. By the late 1930s the institution had been renamed the Seventh-day Adventist Theological Seminary and located at General Conference headquarters in Takoma Park, Maryland. A major step occurred at the autumn 1956 meeting of the General Conference Executive Committee when it decided to establish a university-type institution. The next year witnessed the opening of Potomac University (affectionately known as "PU"), consisting of the theological seminary and a newly organized graduate school. In 1958 the General Conference voted to move the institution to Berrien Springs, Michigan, where, in affiliation with Emmanuel Missionary College, it became Andrews University.

In California, meanwhile, the denomination's College of Medical Evangelists became Loma Linda University on July 1, 1961. Both Andrews and Loma Linda had developed to the level at which they could offer fully accredited academic doctoral degrees by the 1970s. Loma Linda, of course, had been graduating medical doctors since 1914.

The 1980s and beyond saw the creation of Adventist universities in many parts of the world, including such nations as Mexico, Germany, Kenya, Zimbabwe, Argentina, Brazil, Korea, the Philippines, Thailand, and others. Thus many of the denomination's institutions of higher learning are either gearing up to offer master's and doctoral degrees or are already doing so, some in places first entered by Adventism as "primitive" mission fields only a few decades ago.

A third sign of Adventist maturity is a more genuine internationalization of the denomination than has been seen in the past. In part that internationalization has meant that "foreign missionaries" from the United States, Europe, Great Britain, Australia, and South Africa no longer control the work in the newer fields of Adventist labor. Rather, the church has developed indigenous leaders in nearly every area of its far-flung mission program.

The dislocations occasioned by World War II stimulated to some extent the change from "missionary" to indigenous leadership. But the spirit of nationalism that spread throughout the world between 1945 and the late 1960s immensely speeded up the process. As a result, the administrators of geographical sectors of Adventism up through the General Conference divisions generally are indigenous to the regions they lead. That means that Asians direct the work in Asia, Africans the work in Africa, and Latin Americans the work in South and Central America. The leader of each world division is also a vice president of the General Conference. Beyond that, many of the most important positions in the General Conference's central administration are now held by individuals from parts of the world that only a few years ago were still dependent on North American and European leadership.

That type of internationalization is a far cry from the "missionary" mentality largely maintained into the 1950s and 1960s. Accompanying the nationalization of leadership has been unprecedented growth in nearly every area of world Adventism. Thus a second aspect of the internationalization of the denomination has been a rapid increase in the sheer number of adherents. Table 2 provides the membership for each world division as of January 1, 2012.

Table 2

Number of Adventists in Each World Division as of January 1, 2012.

East-Central Africa	2,784,249	South Pacific	423,579
Euro-Africa	178,168	Southern Africa-Indian Ocean	2,857,402
Euro-Asia	121,238	Southern Asia	1,617,190
Inter-American	3,533,069	Southern Asia-Pacific	1,128,546
North American	1,142,039	Trans-European	118,712
Northern Asia-Pacific	659,630	West-Central Africa	878,296
South American	2,037,772		Total: 17,479,890

Another aspect of the denomination's increasing internationalization is a reciprocity in sending "missionaries" between divisions. Whereas a few years ago being a missionary meant going as a European or North American to some non-Christian or non-Protestant land that might be quite primitive, in the twenty-first century it implies working in a place other than one's native land. Thus Africa, Asia, India, and Latin America send "missionaries" to Europe and the United States and even to each other. Of course, Europeans, Australians, Britons, and Americans still serve in other nations, but it is now a two-way street.

"From everywhere to everywhere" has become a familiar phrase in Adventist mission terminology. Since the church now views its mission in global terms, and since people from around the world serve in other countries, the term *interdivisional worker* more aptly describes people who labor for the church in areas other than their nation of origin than does the word *missionary*.

Perhaps the most impressive way to demonstrate the internationalization of Adventism is by the following graph. Figure 2 demonstrates that what was once a North American religion has become a worldwide movement with only a small fraction of its membership in the North American Division.

Figure 2
Distribution of SDA Membership in Relation to North America

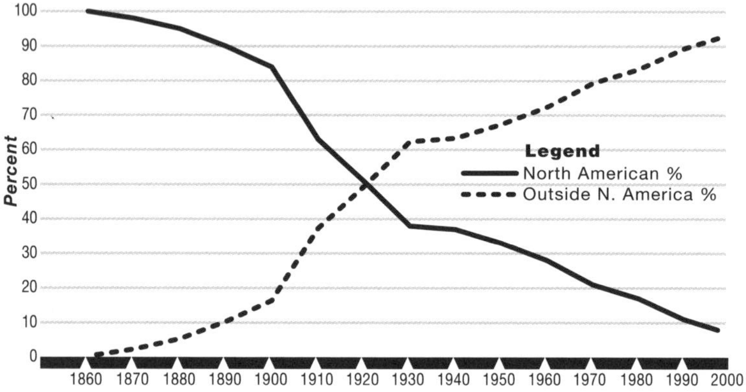

A fourth indication of denominational maturity is size. The church was approaching the 18 million mark in membership by mid-2012. As of January 1, 2011, the church employed 220,760 evangelistic and institutional personnel, and tithes and offerings of over US$2.9 billion supported the work of the church in 2010. That figure does not include funds generated by the denomination's institutions.

As indicated previously, Seventh-day Adventists have taken their institutions wherever they have gone throughout the world. At the beginning of 2011 the church operated 173 hospitals and sanitariums, 168 retirement homes and orphanages, and over 300 clinics and dispensaries. In addition, it had 111 colleges and universities, 1,823 secondary schools, and 5,813 elementary schools. Total enrollment for all levels was 1,668,754. The church also owned and operated 63 publishing houses.

Not only has Adventism grown beyond the wildest dreams of its founders in the late 1840s, but it continues to be one of the most rapidly expanding Christian bodies. Figure 3 indicates the denominational growth curve between 1863 and 2012. Based upon these figures, Adventism could have between 22 and 25 million members by the year 2020.

Figure 3
Growth Curve of SDA Church Between 1863 and 2012
(membership by millions)

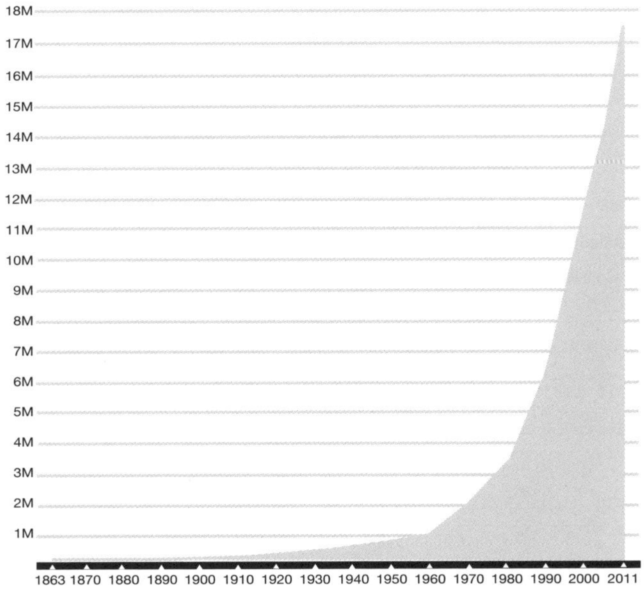

Mission With Conscious Intent

In previous chapters we noted that early Adventists were anything but enthusiastic missionaries. Having begun with an antimission philosophy, they later passively allowed the direction of their mission development to follow the lead of those in other lands who read Adventist publications and then asked for church representatives to visit them. In other words, they had no conscious plan to evangelize the world systematically.

That began to change in the 1890s and in the first half of the twentieth century, but a major shift toward conscious intent took place with the addition of the Department of World Mission and the Seventh-day Adventist Institute of World Mission to the Theological Seminary at Andrews University in 1966. The department teaches classes related to mission, while the institute prepares men and women for cross-cultural service by periodically holding special sessions for new mission appointees. Other functions of the institute have included research and publication on many different aspects of mission and church growth, consultation services on mission outreach, and the planning and conducting of seminars and workshops on mission and growth across cultures.

One of the most conspicuous outgrowths of the heightened consciousness of the need to plan systematically for world mission occurred when the 1990 General Conference session launched Global Mission. Global Mission marks a conscious shift in Adventist missiology as the denomination seeks to complete its mission of preaching the three angels' messages "to every nation, and kindred, and tongue, and people." Adventism has traditionally gauged its mission outreach progress on the "nations" and "tongues" part of that text. Thus as of the beginning of 2011 the Adventist Church had established work in 209 of the 232 nations recognized by the United Nations. That looks good, because the number of people in the small, unentered nations amounts to only some 148,766,000 in a world population of almost 7 billion.

The number of languages serving as a medium for Adventist evangelism is also impressive. As of 2011 that number was 377 for written material and 921 for both written and oral communication.

Global Mission, however, has shifted the denomination's gaze away from those comfortable statistics and toward a new way of looking at denominational mission accountability. Rather than focusing on *nations*, Global Mission places attention on the fact that the Adventist message is to go to "every *kindred*, and *tongue*, and *people*." That approach is much less comforting.

Research tells us that as of 1990 our planet had approximately 5,000 ethnolinguistic or population groupings of 1 million people each. Adventists had at least one church in about 3,200 of those groups. That left approximately 1,800 in which the denomination had absolutely no presence. Those 1,800 groupings represented more than 2 billion people.

Facing such facts, Adventism felt impelled to open its eyes to the magnitude of the task that lay before it. It found itself forced to think of the denomination's tasks in terms of the most difficult areas to reach, not just those that have been receptive.

The goal of the Global Mission program instituted in 1990 was "to establish an Adventist presence in each of the 1,800 untouched groups of 1 million people before A.D. 2000. *That means planting at least one new church every other day in these unreached areas during the next 10 years!*" (Global Mission insert, Adv. Rev., July 5, 1990).

Of course, even that goal was just a beginning point, since we reach people for Christ on a one-to-one basis and not as people groups. On the other hand, it was a place to start. While Global Mission has not reached its impressive goal, it has made major strides forward.

One important spin-off of Global Mission has been a denominational move to face Adventism's mission to the world with more conscious intent than ever before. That consciousness was put into concrete terms beginning in 1990 with the creation of Global Mission Study Centers that focus on Muslim, Jewish, and East Asian religions as well as the secular/postmodern challenge. The year 2010 saw a significant initiative with the establishment of the General Conference Mission Board and the placing of all worldwide mission entities under the direction of the denomination's Secretariat. In the unofficial parachurch realm such organizations as Adventist Frontier Missions, Maranatha Volunteers International, and Adventist-laymen's Services and Industries (ASI) have done much to energize and expand Adventist mission.

The denomination is concerned not merely with evangelizing, but also with the imperative of Christ to feed the hungry and help the sick. Thus it sponsors such humanitarian programs as the Adventist Development and Relief Agency (ADRA). Operating around the world, ADRA helps individuals and communities gain the basic necessities of life, enabling them to become more self-sufficient.

Such humanitarian projects are not divorced from evangelism in its narrower sense. In fact, the denomination's humanitarian activities often act as an entering wedge for Adventist evangelism, since people are often more receptive to those who have cared about them.

Global Mission has utilized many means, both direct and indirect, to reach its goals. One of them is the continued expansion of Adventist World Radio in an effort to blanket the earth with the message of the three angels. Coupled with that effort, the latter part of the 1990s witnessed the denomination begin to utilize Internet technology to spread its message and pursue aggressively the development of a satellite television communication system tied to downlink units in local communities throughout the world. Thus the denomination can now simultaneously reach thousands of local congregations on all continents. The new century has brought a fresh focus on transmitting the biblical message through the creation of the Adventist Television Network, which operates Hope Channels in various languages.

The collapse of the iron curtain also aided Adventist outreach in the early nineties. Seizing the initiative, the Seventh-day Adventist Church moved quickly to establish a theological seminary and a publishing house in Russia. And during the early years of the 1990s hundreds of Seventh-day Adventist ministers and laypersons conducted scores of evangelistic campaigns in various parts of the former Soviet Union and other Eastern European nations. By the end of the decade the church in many former Communist nations had greatly increased its membership. More recently Adventist growth in India and mainland China has surged forward.

All in all, it is an exciting time to be a Seventh-day Adventist. The denomination has some of its greatest challenges right before it. It also, as might be expected, faces some internal tensions.

Challenges as Adventism Faces the Twenty-first Century

We can naturally expect a certain amount of disharmony in any denomination that has almost 18 million members scattered around the world. That has occurred in Adventism, both in its past and its present. Two areas in which the denomination suffers from inner tension in the second decade of the century are the doctrinal and the cultural.

While Adventists around the world share a basic harmony on their 28 fundamental beliefs, discussion—and even sharp disagreement at times—continues on such items as the definition of Christian perfection, the human nature of Christ during His incarnation, the nature of righteousness by faith, proper forms of worship, the role of Ellen White, the interface of science and religion, and certain issues related to the interpretation of inspired materials. While it would be nice to have complete unity in all theological matters, that ideal has never been reached in the history of either Adventism or the larger Christian church.

On the positive side, we should note that the points upon which Adventists agree far outweigh, in both number and importance, those upon which they disagree. Beyond that, if the various factions discuss their differences in the loving spirit of Jesus, they can expect to obtain progressively better theological understandings in the future.

Perhaps the most divisive cultural issue in Adventism in the second decade of the twenty-first century is nationalism. One of the great challenges for world Adventism will be to continue to adjust in a satisfactory manner to a decrease of North American and European dominance in the face of the rapid growth of several of the church's divisions in less developed parts of the world.

Another divisive cultural issue is the role of women in ministry. We noted in chapter 5 that women have always had a part in Adventist ministry. Several were licensed as ministers in the nineteenth century, but apparently none were ever formally ordained, even though the 1881 General Conference session appeared to look favorably on that possibility.

The issue of ordination lay somewhat dormant until the 1970s and 1980s, when larger numbers of women began serving as pastors of Adventist congregations. Since that time the church has had increasing discussion on the topic, eliciting strong feelings on both sides of the issue. In the 1980s a major step occurred when many congregations in the United States and other places began to ordain women as local church elders. That decade also witnessed some female pastors baptizing new members.

On the other hand, the denomination merely "studied," albeit vigorously, the issue of the ordination of women as full gospel ministers during the eighties. At the 1990 General Conference session, however, the ordination of women came up for formal action. The majority vote went against the idea, with sides tending to form along cultural lines. The majority of the delegates from the United States and Western Europe favored ordination, but the powerful voting blocs representing the denomination's Latin American and African divisions overwhelmingly opposed such a move.

The 1990 session, however, did approve the right of "selected" female ministers to perform the marriage ceremony. Thus by 1990 Adventist female pastors had theoretically gained the right to perform all the essential functions of the ordained minister, but without ordination to the gospel ministry.

In spite of the 1990 vote, the ordination issue was far from settled in the minds of many. It arose again at the 1995 General Conference session, when the North American Division petitioned that divisions that so desired be allowed to ordain females as gospel ministers to serve in those divisions. The world church voted the petition down.

But here the church has a topic that refuses to go away. Each of the world divisions is currently restudying women's ordination for discussion in 2014. Underlying that sensitive issue are weighty questions the church has yet to address. What, for example, does it mean to be a world church? Does it demand that all parts of the church must abide by the same set of cultural norms, or is there room for contextualization as the church applies the timeless principles of Christianity to vastly different cultures and ways of thinking? Thus the implications of truly internationalizing has several facets that we have not yet seriously grappled with.

In addition to doctrinal and cultural tensions, Adventism a decade into the twenty-first century faces the problem of an organizational structure that needs to be revised to meet needs, possibilities, and challenges never imagined at the time of the 1901/1903 reorganization. Not only do we see signs that the denomination's massive organizational structure needs to be trimmed, but some (especially in North America) question Adventism's hierarchical structure and urge a congregational polity. On the other hand, to many it seems that the middle ground between the two extremes may be the healthiest position. They argue for an effective organizational structure that captures the best of both local initiative and the ability to focus the energies of a unified global church in the continuing pursuit of Adventism's mission to the world.

The recently voted option of a union of churches structure, which does away with the need for local conferences and missions, may provide part of the solution.

Beyond tensions over church structure, all religious movements struggle against the temptation of both members and institutions to secularize. Thus renewal and reform on several levels are important issues on the current Adventist agenda. As in 1861 to 1863 and 1901 to 1903, however, moves toward renewal and reform should have as their aim enabling the denomination to become more functional in its mission of carrying the message of the three angels to all the world.

Another topic of concern to many Adventists in the new century is the topic of the delay of the Second Advent. Some in their dismay seek to blame others (often the leaders) for the fact that Christ has not yet come. Other members appear to be lulled into indifference, while still others want to revise or reject the denomination's understanding of apocalyptic prophecy. Perhaps the most widespread problem facing many Adventists in the area of the Second Coming is their tendency to be drawn to the sensational. The path of excitement seeking has proved to be much more to their liking than Jesus' admonition to faithfully watch, wait, and work for the kingdom (see Matt. 24:36-25:46). The church of the twenty-first century, as did the early disciples, needs to wrestle with what Christ meant when He said, "Occupy till I come" (Luke 19:13). Developing a belief that balances Advent faith with healthy "occupation" will be an ongoing challenge until the Advent itself.

Infinite Possibilities

In current Adventism we, as individual members, can choose to focus on either the problems or the possibilities of the church. In that situation we are no different from our predecessors in the 1840s, the 1880s, the 1950s—or in Bible times, for that matter.

Of course, if James White, Joseph Bates, A. G. Daniells, and others had focused merely on the problems, there would be no Seventh-day Adventist Church today. While it is important to face problems responsibly, it is equally important that we do so in a positive and upbuilding manner—one that expresses the faith and hope of Moses, Paul, Luther, and the Adventist founders.

I would like to suggest, as we near the end of this brief history, that each of us has now moved into the stream of that history. History is much more than something that happened a long time ago—it is a current reality, and each of us is an actor in its ongoing flow. Daily we each cast a vote, act a part in a continuing drama.

The Christian view of history is not circular but linear. Earthly history had a beginning at Creation, and it will have an ending at the second coming of Jesus. All of the Bible points to that ending. Adventists have consistently believed that they have a special part to play in that event as the denomination's members preach the message of the three angels of Revelation 14 "to every nation, and kindred, and tongue, and people." Immediately after the preaching of those messages in the Apocalypse comes the great "harvest" that has motivated Seventh-day Adventism for 170 years. Thus Adventism has always been a movement of faith and hope, with a vision of infinite possibilities.

It is that vision that continues to carry the Advent message to the far corners of the earth. As individual members, each of us has an exciting part to play in the "finishing of the work" as we "live expecting and working for the coming of the day of God" (2 Peter 3:12, Phillips).

And as we proceed with the ongoing tasks of the Adventist Church, it is helpful to recall frequently the words of Ellen White, who wrote: "*In reviewing our past history, . . . I can say, Praise God! As I see what the Lord has wrought, I am filled with astonishment, and with confidence in Christ as leader. We have nothing to fear for the future, except as we shall forget the way the Lord has led us, and His teaching in our past history*" (LS 196; italics supplied).

For Those Who Would Like to Read More

Dybdahl, Jon L., ed. *Adventist Mission in the Twenty-first Century: The Joys of Presenting Jesus to a Diverse World.* Hagerstown, Md.: Review and Herald, 1999.

Greenleaf, Floyd. *In Passion for the World.* Pp. 353-459.

Johnsson, William G. *The Fragmenting of Adventism: Ten Issues Facing the Church Today: Why the Next Five Years Are Crucial.* Boise, Idaho: Pacific Press, 1995.

Knight, George R. *If I Were the Devil.* Pp. 19-65, 163-198, 233-269.

———. "Historical and Theological Introduction to the Annotated Edition." *Seventh-day Adventists Answer Questions on Doctrine*, annotated ed. Berrien Springs, Mich.: Andrews University Press, 2003. Pp. xiii-xxvi.

———. *Organizing for Mission and Growth.* Pp. 158-185.

———. *Reading Ellen White: How to Understand and Apply Her Writings.* Hagerstown, Md.: Review and Herald, 1997.

———. *A Search for Identity.* Pp. 160-205.

Land, Gary, ed. *Adventism in America.* Pp. 144-146, 151-154, 171-190.

Schwarz, Richard W., and Floyd Greenleaf. *Light Bearers.* Pp. 339-655.

Vyhmeister, Nancy, ed. *Women in Ministry.* Pp. 235-258, 417-432.

Weeks, Howard B. *Adventist Evangelism in the Twentieth Century.* Pp. 246-309.

Index

Index